# OUR HUNGRY EARTH

# OUR HUNGRY EARTH

## The World Food Crisis

LAURENCE PRINGLE

MACMILLAN PUBLISHING CO., INC.
New York
COLLIER MACMILLAN PUBLISHERS
London

The author wishes to thank Dr. Dana Dalrymple, Agricultural Economist, U.S. Department of Agriculture, for reading and suggesting changes in the manuscript of this book.



Macmillan Publishing Co., Inc.
866 Third Avenue, New York, N.Y. 10022
Collier Macmillan Canada, Ltd.
Printed in the United States of America
10 9 8 7 6 5 4 3 2 1

LIBRARY OF CONGRESS CATALOGING IN PUBLICATION DATA
Pringle, Laurence P
Our hungry earth.
(Science for survival series)
Biblography: p.
Includes index.
SUMMARY: Discusses food supplies, population growth, agricultural advances, and natural resources as aspects of the world food crisis.
1. Food supply—Juvenile literature. 2. Population—Juvenile literature. 3. Natural resources—Juvenile literature. [1. Food supply. 2. Population. 3. Natural resources] I. Title.
HD9000.5.P7 338.1′9 76–10828
ISBN 0–02–775290–9

# CONTENTS

# OUR HUNGRY EARTH

# CHAPTER ONE

# More Mouths to Feed

More than 215,000 children are born every day—that's almost 80 million a year. In 1975, 4 billion people lived on earth. That is 4 billion people who need living space, food, and other resources. No two of them are alike, and yet they can all be lumped together in one way: they are simply 4 billion mouths to feed.

"A mouth to feed"—an odd way to think of a person. The phrase tells you nothing about a person's appearance or work or dreams. But it may be useful to pause and think about everyone, including your family and friends, as "mouths to feed." People in the United States and other rich industrial nations tend to forget that most of humankind is preoccupied, day in and day out, with the task of getting enough food to eat.

There is nothing new about famine, starvation, or simply going to bed hungry. Probably there has never been a time when everyone has been well-fed. Never before, however,

---

"We're expecting a few extra people for dinner."

has the world food situation seemed so serious a threat to the well-being of all people on earth, rich and poor alike.

Ever since agriculture was first developed, the earth's food production has increased. But human numbers have also grown. Often there have been crop failures or wars which caused widespread hunger and famine in some nations.

In 436 B.C., thousands of Romans reportedly threw themselves into the Tiber River rather than slowly starve to death. Perhaps the most famous famine occurred in Ireland, beginning in 1846, when a blight struck that nation's basic food, the potato. An estimated 1½ million people starved to death.

The first modern food crisis occurred when drought struck most of Asia during 1965 and 1966. Wheat shipments to India from the United States prevented what might have been one of the worst famines in history. Public attention was focused on world food production, and the picture was a gloomy one. In 1967, two food experts wrote a book called *Famine 1975!*

Others were more optimistic. And before long, their outlook seemed confirmed. Food production began to increase faster than population growth. A "Green Revolution" was underway; new varieties of wheat and rice were yielding larger crops than the old varieties of these grains. By the early 1970s, newspaper headlines read "Asian Countries Fear a Rice Glut" and "Fear of Famine Lessens in World."

The optimistic headlines were soon replaced with news of crop failures, famines, and disappearing grain reserves. A new wave of alarm swept the world. Was *Famine 1975!* coming true?

The world food situation is a complex one, involving pol-

itics, economics, weather, and many other factors. This complexity is best illustrated by the food crisis of 1972–1974. It began with the failure of the 1972 grain crop in the Soviet Union. In the past, the Soviet Union had made up occasional shortages of wheat and other grains by killing off young livestock, thus saving its limited grain for people rather than feeding it to cows and hogs. But by the 1970s it had become government policy to put more meat and dairy products on Soviet tables. In 1972, therefore, the Soviet Union chose to make up its grain deficit through imports. It also cut its usual grain exports to Eastern European nations, and these countries had to look elsewhere for wheat and other grains.

Together, the Soviet Union and Eastern European nations imported about 30 million metric tons of grain during 1972–1973. (A metric ton weighs 2,200 pounds.) Most of this grain was bought from the United States and Canada, which for many years had stored surplus grain.

Since 1960, the world's grain reserves have ranged from about 155 million metric tons to 100 million metric tons. A hundred million metric tons may seem like a lot of grain, but it represents less than a month's supply for the earth.

The Soviet grain purchases of 1972–1973 reduced the world's grain reserves, and they dropped even lower because of events in 1974. Drought caused poor crops in India and other developing nations. The United States had its worst growing season in a quarter of a century. Grain reserves fell to a new low, and prices for the available grain reached new highs. Developing nations (sometimes called "less developed" or "poor" nations) paid twice as much to import American grain in 1974 as they had in 1972. Some countries could not afford to buy enough food for their starving peoples.

Because of the worldwide energy crisis, the price of oil, gasoline, and natural gas also rose during this period. It cost more to run tractors and irrigation pumps and to transport farm supplies and grain, and this affected the cost of raising food. Developing nations were faced with higher prices for desperately needed food, fuel, and fertilizer. Higher prices also caused a decline in the amount of aid in food and fertilizer from the U.S. government and from private agencies such as CARE.

Grain prices dropped somewhat in the following year, but the food crisis of 1972–1974 raised some disturbing questions: Was the crisis avoidable? Had government policies

contributed to it? What changes could be made to avoid another such crisis?

A close look at the world in the early 1970s shows that demand for food grew because of increasing population *and* because of changing diets in developed countries. People in the United States, Japan, Europe, and the Soviet Union had been increasing the amount of meat in their diets. This added greatly to the grain needs of these countries, since an animal must be fed between three and ten pounds of grain in order to produce a pound of meat.

Most people in developing nations make most of their meals directly from grains. They eat an average of 400 pounds of grain a year. In contrast, a person in the United States uses almost a ton of grain each year. Only about 200

pounds are eaten directly in such foods as cereal and bread. The rest is fed to animals and comes to us indirectly in the form of meat, milk, cheese, and eggs. This is a very inefficient use of the food energy in grains, yet grain-exporting nations, especially the United States, have promoted the use of grain to feed livestock all over the world.

From television or newspaper reports on the world food situation, you might suppose that there is a terrible scarcity of food in the world today, and that this is because of the needs of the populous developing nations. This is simply not true. Each year livestock in the United States eat as much grain as all the people in China and India combined. Developed nations make up only a third of the earth's population, but they consume two-thirds of its food.

There is plenty of food; it is just spread around very unevenly and used very inefficiently. Recognizing that fact, however, does not solve the world food problem. Few people in developed nations are willing to change their diets so that those in developing nations can eat better. Even if they were, a complicated (and expensive) program for distributing food around the world would have to be set up.

The food crisis of 1972–1974 raised fundamental questions about the agricultural policies of the United States and other grain-exporting nations. During the late 1960s, there was fear of huge grain surpluses in the United States and Canada. Good harvests all over the world would mean low demand for exports, and that would mean low prices for farmers and added costs for storing surplus grain. Accordingly, the United States and Canada reduced the amount of acreage planted to grain.

For many years the governments of the United States, Canada, and Australia paid some farmers *not* to grow certain crops rather than have them add to large surpluses. As late as 1972, one acre was held out of production for every four and a half acres planted and harvested in the United States. These payments came to a halt in 1974.

Because of crop surpluses, the U.S. government had encouraged other nations to depend on it for emergency food, either through purchase or gift. This helped get rid of bothersome surpluses, but it had another effect. Developing nations "knew" they could rely on imported food. So leaders in these nations often encouraged industrial development rather than food production. The aid of developed countries usually favored industrial projects too. By the

1970s, about one person out of every ten in developing nations depended on imported grain for some of his or her diet.

During the 1972–1974 food crisis, however, developing nations discovered the folly of their dependence on imported food. Millions of people, mostly in the poorest countries, were dropped from food-aid programs of the United States. Even some of the more developed nations were rudely surprised. In 1973, the United States, source of 85 percent of

In the 1960s, American grain reserves filled huge storage bins to capacity. Such surpluses are a thing of the past.

all soybeans entering the world market, suddenly halted soybean exports in order to help reduce food prices at home. This came as a shock to Japan and other countries that were big users of imported soybeans.

The 1972–1974 food crisis taught a bitter lesson: no nation should depend indefinitely on others for its basic food supply. The world food situation is delicately balanced. A crop failure in any major food-exporting country can send shock waves of shortages and soaring prices all over the earth.

The food crisis of the early 1970s began to change our approach to this problem. The fact that developing nations needed to produce more of their own food was recognized. Efforts were made to set up a world food reserve. And people in developed nations began wondering about some moral questions: Was it right to eat, and waste, great amounts of meat while fellow passengers on Spaceship Earth could barely get enough rice or wheat to survive? Should fertilizers be spread lavishly on lawns and golf courses when they could make a critical difference in the amount of food produced in another nation?

Most of us have seen television pictures of starving children. Perhaps because of these pictures, perhaps for other reasons, people are becoming more concerned about feeding everyone on earth. Like the problems of pollution and energy, the problem of food is a global one. We have learned that decisions and events on the other side of the earth can affect us. To ignore them is short-sighted and foolish. It is something like saying to a fellow passenger in a lifeboat, "Your end of the boat is sinking."

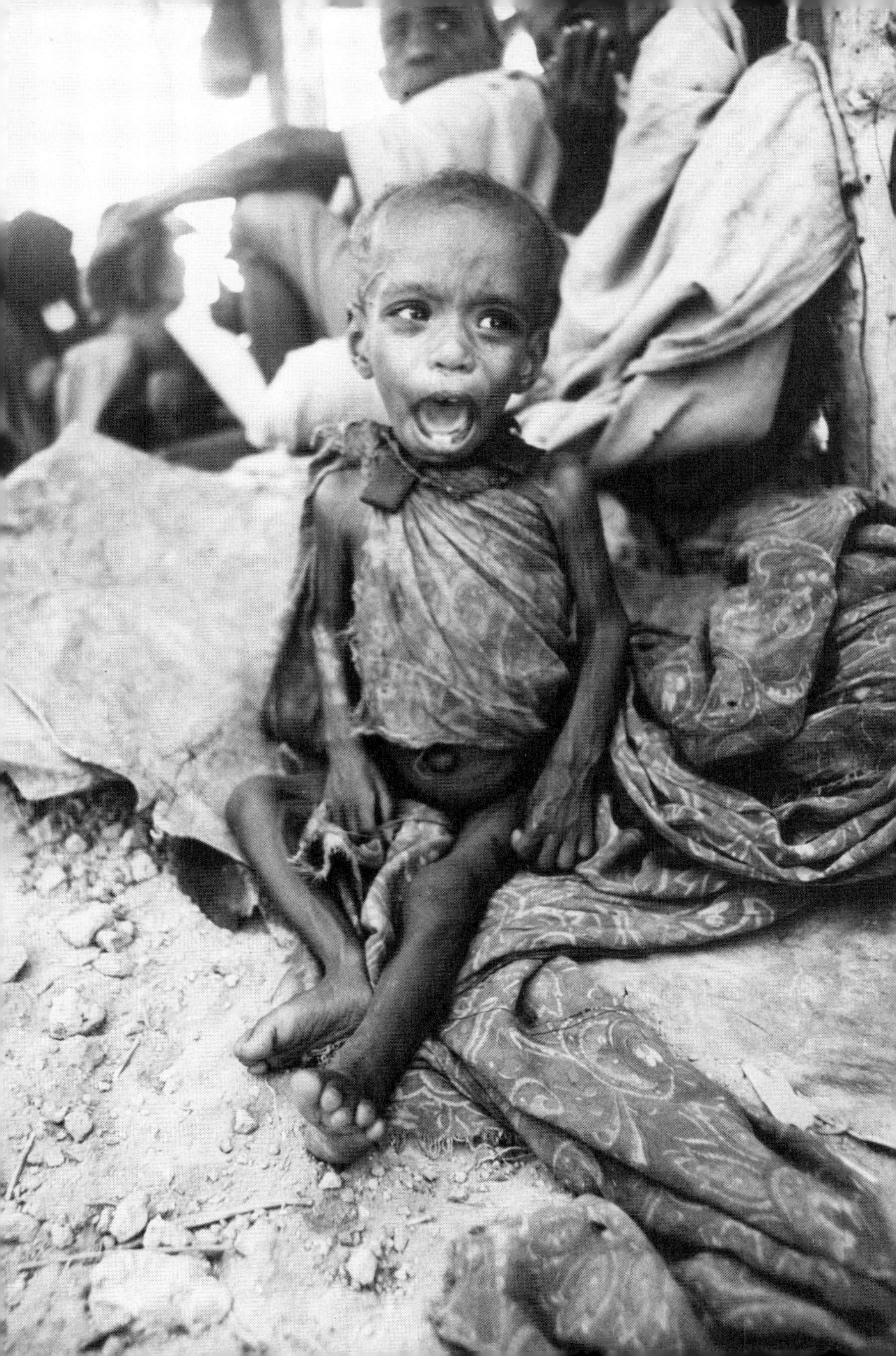

Kellogg's
RAISIN
MILK
HEALTHIEST
BARGAIN
YOU CAN BUY
PASTEURIZED PROCESS CHEESE SPREAD
GRAND UNION
SALTINE
Have You
Weighed the
Difference?
ScotTowels

## CHAPTER TWO

# Food and Famine

We know a lot about good nutrition—what people need to eat in order to be healthy and resist disease. But *providing* good nutrition for all the people on earth is another matter. Hundreds of millions of people suffer from a lack of food, or from not enough good food.

Each of us needs a certain amount of food and certain kinds of food every day. We get energy mainly from fats and carbohydrates (sugar and starch). Protein is chiefly a body-building substance. Skin, muscles, bones, and all the other parts of our bodies are made up of protein compounds. We need protein for growth, repair, and maintenance of our bodies. And vitamins and minerals are important too. In India, an estimated 15 million people are partly or totally blind because of a lack of vitamin A. A person who consistently lacks vitamins, minerals, or protein is often said to be *malnourished.*

The energy in foods we eat is measured in calories (actually kilocalories). This is the amount of energy needed to raise the temperature of one kilogram of water by one degree

Celsius. The amount of energy that people need varies a lot. An active man weighing 150 pounds might need 3,000 calories a day. A less active man of the same weight might need only 2,000. The U.S. average for men is 2,700 calories a day. A person who consistently lacks enough calories is usually called *undernourished.*

We know very little about the calorie needs of people in developing countries. Many adults in these nations weigh less than 150 pounds each, but they may do a lot of hard work, which requires many calories. The average daily need of a person in South Asia is 1,900 calories, according to the Food and Agricultural Organization (FAO) of the United Nations. Studies of very poor people in Chile, Brazil, and India show that they survive on as little as 1,500 to 1,700 calories a day.

The number of calories eaten is a measure of an adequate diet, but the amount and kinds of protein we eat are an important measure of the *quality* of our food. For example, proteins are vital for normal development of our bodies and brains. Proteins are made up of about twenty different chemical compounds called amino acids. Our bodies are able to make twelve of these amino acids by combining chemicals from various foods. But the remaining eight of these vital "building blocks" cannot be made by humans and must come directly from the foods we eat.

When one or more essential amino acids are missing, many of the others cannot be used by our bodies. We need certain amounts of all amino acids, usually during the same meal, so that they can be reassembled by our bodies into all the different kinds of protein. All eight essential amino acids are present in chicken eggs. The protein in animal foods—milk, cheese, meat, and fish—is also of high quality.

Plant foods contain lesser amounts of protein and lack key amino acids. Peas, beans, soybeans, and nuts are the plant foods richest in protein, while tubers (such as potatoes) contain the least. Nevertheless, a combination of plant foods can give us all the amino acids we need. For centuries the Chinese have eaten a type of cabbage which provides the amino acids that are missing in their staple food, rice.

THE FOUR BASIC FOOD GROUPS

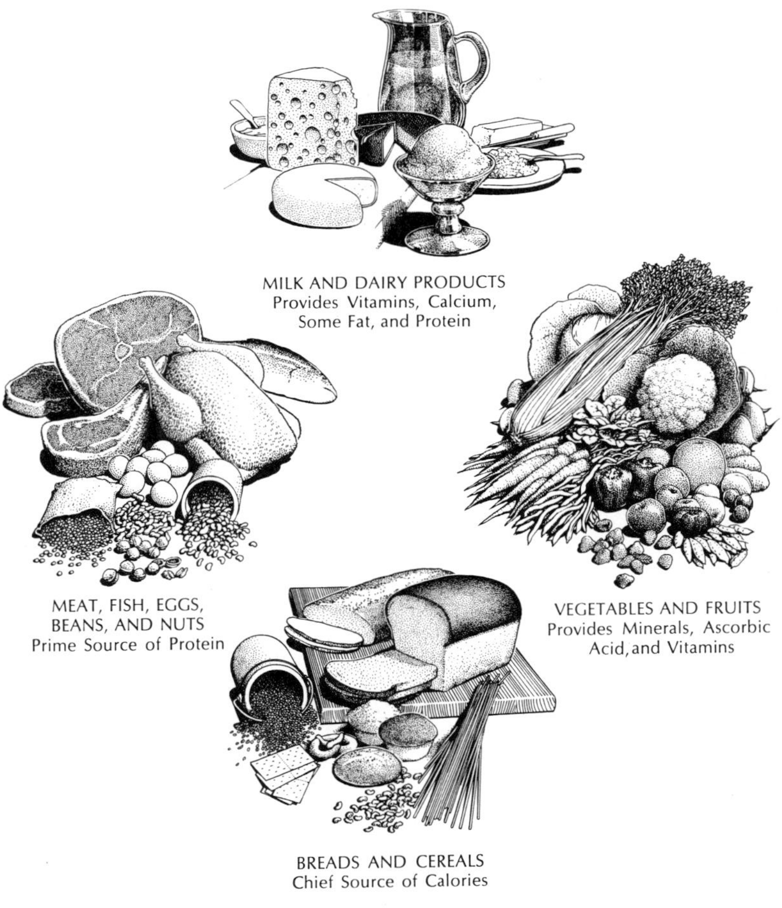

The importance of the essential amino acids becomes clear when you see children who lack them in their diets. They often have swollen bellies, peeling skin, and discolored hair. These are the symptoms of a disease called kwashiorkor. Kwashiorkor is an African word, but the disease has had many names all over the world. In Jamaica, children with kwashiorkor were called "sugar babies." They got plenty of

Malnourished children—a brother and sister in India

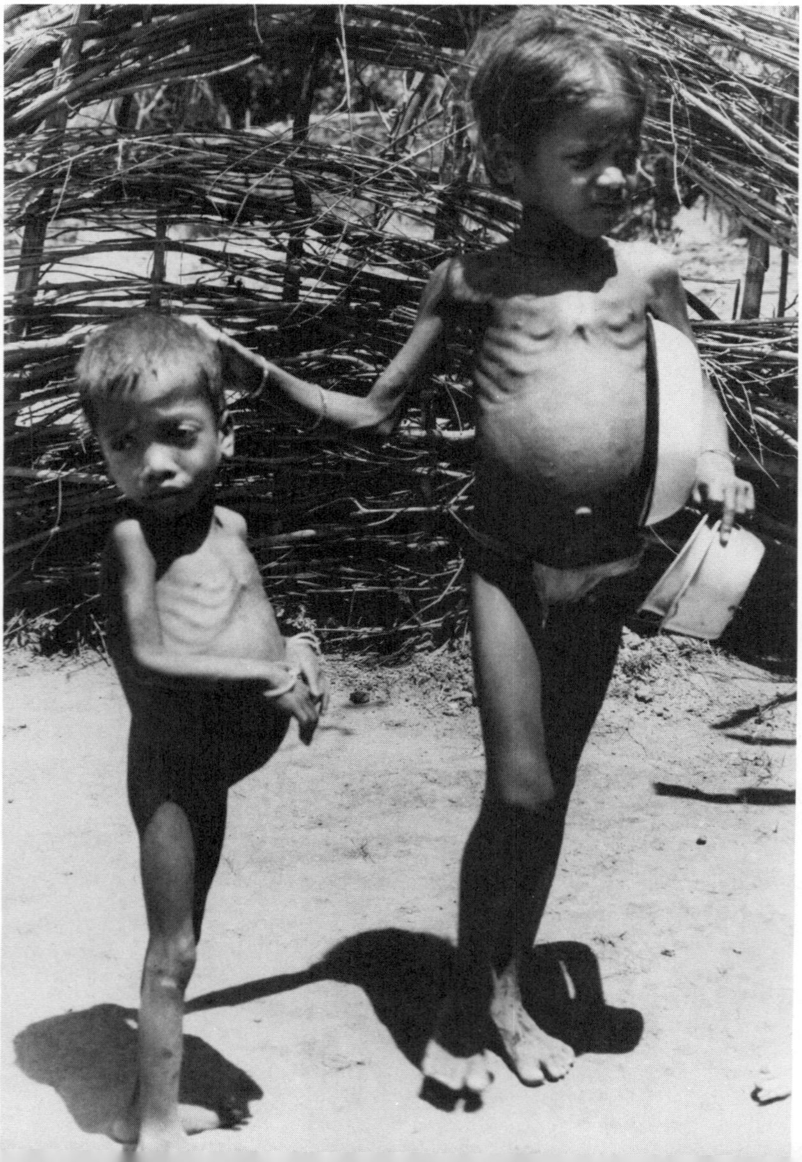

calories (but no protein) from sugar, and people used to think that sugar itself caused the disease. In developing nations, kwashiorkor develops frequently in babies soon after they are weaned. They get enough protein as long as they are breast-fed, but then the solid foods that replace the milk leave them protein-starved.

A doctor who spent several years in Thailand found that breast-feeding was still the custom in rural areas. He saw little malnutrition among young children there. In the slums of Bangkok, however, most women stopped breast-feeding within six months of their child's birth. The doctor found that well over half of the babies were malnourished, and as many as 15 percent suffered from a disease called maramus, caused by too little protein *and* too few calories.

Unfortunately, breast-feeding is going "out of fashion" among women who live in urban areas of developing nations.

Manufacturers of substitutes (cow's milk formulas) for infants advertise their products in developing nations. They hire nurses to visit hospitals and homes, and urge new mothers to bottle-feed their babies. But this is one modern convenience that people would be better off without. Usually a poor family cannot afford to buy an adequate amount of the formula. Often the package instructions are not understood. The formula may be mixed with unclean water or may be served in an unclean bottle. Such practices lead to diseases that the child may be too weak to resist.

This is a tragic development. Human milk is ideal for human infants. It usually provides all of a child's nutritional needs for the first four to six months of life, and up to three-quarters of its needs to the twelfth month or beyond. Human breast milk is worth millions of dollars in good nutrition to developing nations.

In much of Asia, Africa, and Latin America, half of all people who die are children under six years of age. Often the official cause of death is measles, diarrhea, or some other not-so-serious disease—but the underlying cause is a poor diet which leaves children too weak to resist disease. Death from measles is much more common in poor nations than in rich ones. In a study of child deaths in several Guatemalan villages, for example, while the official cause of death was listed as parasitic worms, nearly 40 percent of the victims were found to have kwashiorkor.

In developing nations, the children who live past the age of six have not necessarily escaped disease or malnutrition. They have just *survived.* Often they are permanently affected by their ordeal. If a child's brain develops poorly because of a lack of protein, it stays that way for life, regardless of later diet. No amount of protein, education, or other aid can undo the damage done during the critical early years of development.

A combination of malnutrition and undernutrition often produces adults who are smaller and more lightweight than normal. The average Bengal man (in India) weighs only about a hundred pounds.

Stunted bodies and minds, dying children—these are some of the costs of being poor in many developing nations. However, it is a mistake to assume that some nations are well-fed and others are not. Even in the poorest nations, part of the population is well-fed. And you can find malnutrition anywhere, even in the richest nations on earth. A Senate Committee on Nutrition recently estimated that 6 percent of the people in the United States suffer from malnutrition. As one food scientist expressed it, "those with money eat well wherever they may be, while the poor, be they in Bangladesh or Boston, suffer."

The suffering is most savage during a famine—a severe food shortage throughout an entire nation or region. Serious famines have occurred during nearly every year since World War II. There will be more famines, and probably more severe ones, in the future.

A famine usually begins with widespread crop failure. The poor harvest may be caused by drought, floods, crop pests or diseases, the effects of war, or a combination of factors. Without food, the body uses stored fat for energy. People get very thin even though their bellies may be bloated with water. Their heartbeat slows, and their skin becomes dull, gray,

and paperlike. People die of some "mild" disease, or because the heart or digestive system stops working.

Children and older persons die first. Usually there is large-scale panic. People hurry, as best they can, toward food supplies, or rumored food supplies. Families become separated and children lost. Young adults and adolescents may form roaming bandit groups. Epidemics of disease spread explosively and take a great toll of the weakened people. The famine also destroys much of the region's livestock, and the people are forced to eat the seeds that would otherwise be used for planting next year's crops, making later recovery all the more difficult.

In the early 1970s a famine occurred in the six-nation Sahel (Arabic for "border" or "fringe") area south of the Sahara in Africa. It demonstrated all the horrors of famine, and also showed how well-intentioned efforts to help developing nations may do more harm than good.

The Sahel is a semidesert region, with only four months of rain a year. The countries there—Senegal, Mauritania, Mali, Upper Volta, Niger, and Chad—were once French colonies. (The Sahel region also extends into the Sudan and Ethiopia.) Most of the people live in villages and raise grains like millet and sorghum for food. Nomads also roam the land, living with their herds of cattle, camels, and goats.

During the 1960s, foreign aid programs from rich, developed nations gave Sahelian people better health care. The human population grew rapidly because fewer people died of diseases. More and more people tried to farm the land.

War refugees put a great strain on available food supplies.

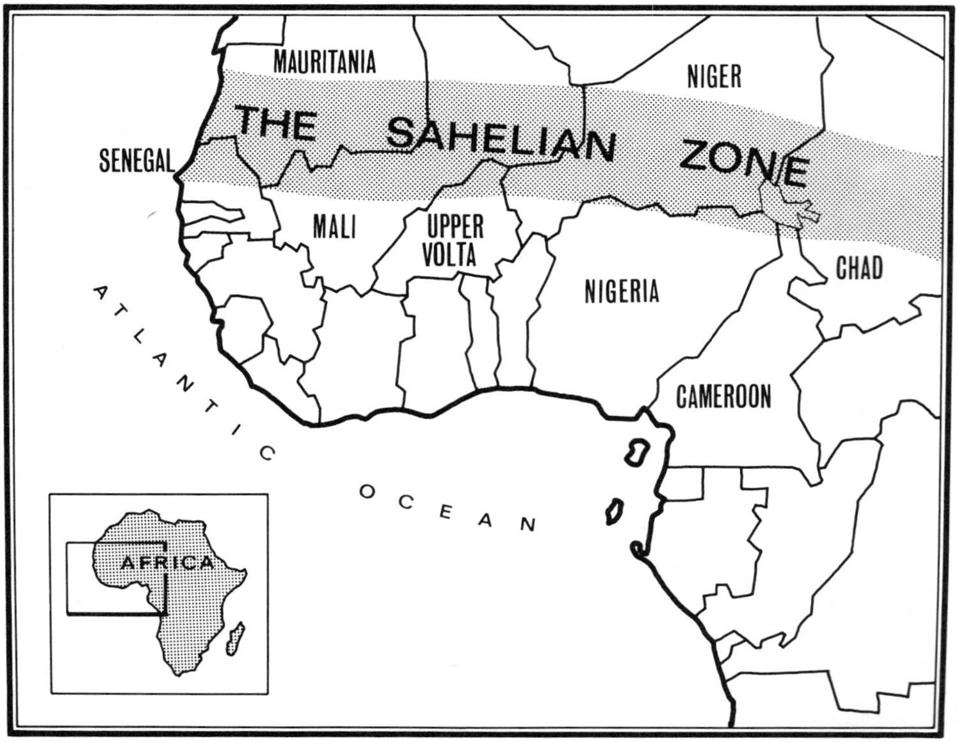


They were encouraged to grow peanuts and cotton, as exportable cash crops, on their best land. For food crops they used poorer soils. But these soils could not support intensive farming for long. Soil fertility declined rapidly.

Aid to Sahelian nations also included the drilling of thousands of water wells. Traditionally, the nomads had kept only as many cattle as they could water by hand from a few scattered wells. The livestock population had been kept in check by a limited water supply. New wells and water pumps changed all that. Between 1960 and 1971 the number of cattle grew from about 18 million to 25 million.

Disaster was inevitable, but it was delayed by seven years of unusually high rainfall. Even then, the fragile land took a beating from overgrazing and farming. The Sahel was already sick when a drought began in 1968. As the grasses died, herdsmen cut down trees so that their cattle could eat the leaves. The drought continued, and the grasslands and farmers' fields started turning to desert. By 1972, cattle and people began dying in large numbers. By the end of 1974, an estimated 100,000 people and 5 million cattle had died.

After several years of drought, the undernourished children of a tribe in northern Chad were threatened with a disease called diphtheria. The tribe's leaders asked that no medicine be sent. It was better, they explained, for their children to die quickly from disease than slowly from starvation.

Many of those who died in the Sahel were nomadic herdspeople. Emergency foods were delayed in reaching them because of a lack of good roads. There was also a lack of planning for emergency relief, even though there had been

advance warnings of the worsening conditions in the Sahel.

The Sahelian drought was caused by a change in global weather patterns. Monsoon rains shifted southward. (Monsoons are the dominant winds of a region; there are dry monsoons and wet monsoons.) This change also caused droughts in parts of India and Latin America. But the shift in climate cannot be blamed entirely for the growing desert of the Sahel. True, the Sahara has been advancing southward at the rate of thirty miles per year in some areas. However, one large Sahelian ranch, fenced in and lightly grazed, remained green while the surrounding land became desert. The southward march of the Sahara may have been helped along by drought, but the major cause of desertification was the abuse of the land by people and the overgrazing by cattle.

Because of mistakes made in the Sahel, people there will need food aid for many years. Restoration of the land will require large amounts of money—and common sense. Somehow, the people of the Sahel must be brought back to a sound ecological relationship with their fragile land of limited resources.

The Sahelian tragedy was an unusual case in some ways, but there is no reason to expect an end to famines. There *is* reason to expect them to get worse. In many developing nations, droughts and poor harvests are not abnormal; they are the rule rather than the exception. Even the most optimistic food experts say this. Still, they disagree about the seriousness of the world food situation.

---

The nomadic life of many people in the Sahel ended when their livestock died.

Perhaps it is time to say something about food experts, and experts in general. Like all humans, they differ in their outlook on life: some like to "view with alarm," others prefer a more rosy view. Their outlook may also be influenced by the organizations they work for. Employees of the United States Department of Agriculture tend to be optimistic about solving world food problems. Those of the Food and Agricultural Organization of the United Nations tend to be more pessimistic. And all food experts face a common problem: the information they work with is often incomplete and inaccurate.

An FAO survey in 1963 estimated that two-thirds of the earth's people suffered from undernutrition or malnutrition or both. Many food experts doubted the accuracy of this gloomy report, and the FAO was accused of exaggerating the world's food problems. Of course, it *is* difficult to get accurate information about the diets of people in developing nations.

In 1974, the FAO estimated that about 460 million people had "insufficient protein-energy supply." Thus, with a wave of a statistical wand, the number of people with serious food problems had been reduced from billions to millions. The FAO's new figures are considered more accurate than earlier ones, but at least one prominent food expert considers them to be too low. Lester R. Brown, once administrator of the International Development Service of the U.S. Department of Agriculture, and now President of Worldwatch Institute, says, "Probably a billion or more people suffer from serious hunger or malnutrition, at least during part of the year."

Although food experts may argue about the exact dimensions of the world food problem, they agree that it is one of the greatest challenges facing humankind, and that actions taken in the next few years will have a vital effect on the quality of life for all people in the twenty-first century.

Food aid is discussed by members of the Food and Agricultural Organization of the United Nations.

# CHAPTER THREE

## The Power of Population

Imagine a highway of grain, 55½ feet high and 6 feet deep, stretching completely around the earth's equator. This is the amount of grain we use each year, about 1.2 billion metric tons. But unlike other highways, this road of grain must be rebuilt every year. And each year we must add 625 miles of the same width and depth. This represents the 30 million metric tons needed to provide food for the annual increase in population.

These imaginary highways of food were described by Dr. Norman E. Borlaug, winner of the 1970 Nobel Peace Prize for his work in developing high-yield varieties of wheat. He is not optimistic that necessary steps will be taken to increase food production or to hold down what he calls "monstrous" population growth. And, he says, it is not a matter of doing one or the other; food output will *never* be adequate unless population growth slows and eventually stops.

This is part of a theory put forth by Thomas Malthus, an

A hospital nursery in France, a nation whose population is nearly stable

English economist of the late eighteenth and early nineteenth centuries. In 1798 he published his famous *Essay on the Principle of Population.* Malthus believed that the population of any region or country (or the world) must ultimately be brought into line with its resources—either through human effort to regulate the population or through catastrophes such as famine. Malthus also suggested that food production would limit human populations because the number of people grew so much faster than food supplies—"the power of population is indefinitely greater than the power in the earth to produce subsistence for man."

Malthus' ideas get plenty of attention whenever the world food situation seems to get worse. So far his theories have not come true. In his time, the resources available for food production were land, water, and labor provided by humans and animals. He could not foresee the use of gasoline, natural

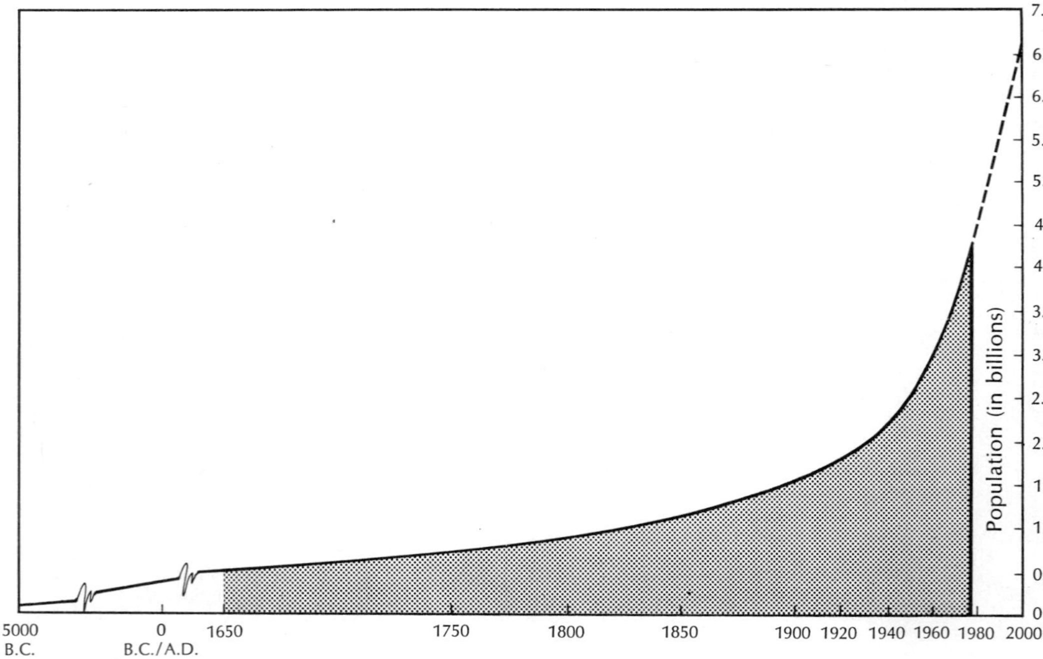


WORLD POPULATION GROWTH

gas, and other fossil fuels. We use energy from these fuels to make and operate farm equipment; make and apply fertilizers, insect poisons, and other farm chemicals; pump water; and transport goods to and from farms. Malthus also did not foresee our great increase in knowledge about raising livestock and crops. Resources like these have enabled us to increase food output at the same rate as population growth. Thus "the power in the earth to produce subsistence for man" is much greater than Malthus imagined.

World food output has risen steadily. And, according to most food experts, we still have quite a few tricks up our

food-production sleeve. But this cannot go on indefinitely. The resources of the earth *are* limited, and so, therefore, are food supplies and the numbers of people who can be fed. No one knows what the upper limits may be. When they are reached, at least part of Thomas Malthus' theory will have come true—the human population will be held in check by its resources.

There is danger, however, that a combination of growing population and severe crop failures will bring the starvation and famine that Malthus predicted sooner than we expect. Before we run out of resources, we may run out of time in which to develop them.

Since 1950, the world's population has been growing at the rate of nearly 2 percent a year. At that rate, it will double in just thirty-five years. By the year 2000, it is expected to reach 6 billion, perhaps 7 billion. This growth rate is much faster than the one that has been normal for most of human history. It cannot continue for long—there will not be enough food or other resources to go around. Somehow the growth rate must return to normal—close to zero—within a few generations.

The yearly increase in world population occurs mostly in the developing nations. Mexico contributes more to world population growth than the United States and Canada combined. About 40 percent of the annual increase comes from two countries, mainland China and India. In the next twenty-five years, more than 90 percent of the earth's population increase will occur in developing nations. The future course of human population—and the quality of life on earth—depends on what happens in these countries.

Some nations, including Brazil, still regard a fast-growing

population as an asset, and they encourage people to have large families. Other nations have advocated smaller families for many years. The Mexican government opposed birth control for decades but now has a family-planning program. Bangladesh raised the legal age for marriage in order to help lower its birth rate. The governments of the Philippines and Singapore use their tax systems to try to discourage people from having large families.

Much more can be done to educate people about how to limit births, and to make birth-control devices widely available at low cost. But this is only one step toward reducing population growth rates. It is probably much less vital than many people think.

The greatest obstacle to slowing population growth is the simple desire of some people to have many children. Having birth-control devices and information does not change this desire. In the Philippines, for example, the government set up a model birth-control program, supported in part by the United States Agency for International Development (AID). After five years, however, the population continued to grow at the high rate of 3 percent a year. In India, more than twenty years of government family-planning programs failed to reduce that nation's growth rate significantly.

Only in the Indian state of Kerala has the birth rate fallen markedly. Compared with other states, its people are well-educated and well-fed. Its infant death rate is the lowest in the country. Alas, Kerala is not the same as all of India. In other states, people expect some of their offspring to die. Since the people depend on children, especially sons, for security in their old age, they believe that they must have at least six children in order to have one son survive to adult-

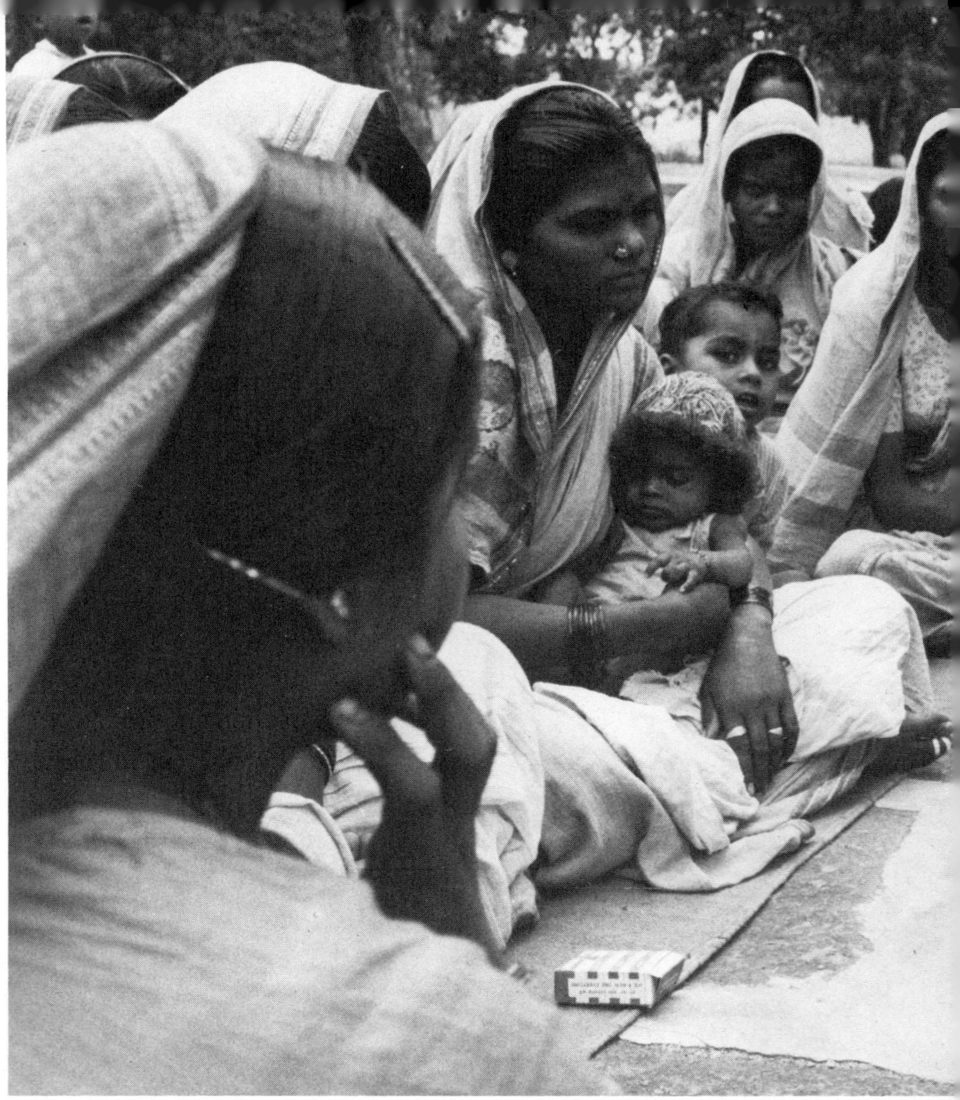

hood. No wonder family-planning slogans such as "Stop at two" seem like nonsense to them.

History shows that people can change their attitudes and decide that fewer children are sufficient. If enough people change their minds, then the population growth rate slows. This has happened in England, Western Europe, the Soviet Union, the United States, and other industrialized nations. In many of these countries, the decline in population growth

In India, information about reproduction and birth control methods is available, but most people still believe that they need to have many children.

occured long before modern birth-control methods were invented or were legal. Once people believed it was in their best interest to have smaller families, they managed to do just that.

To reach their present low growth rates, the developed nations went through a series of changes called a demographic transition. All of the earth's developing nations are expected to do the same. Population experts disagree, however, on the causes of these vital changes, and on how we might assist a nation like India through its demographic transition.

According to demographers (scientists who study human populations), there are three stages in a demographic transition. The first stage held true for most of human history. In this stage, there are high death rates and high birth rates. Many infants and children die, and adults can only expect to live to be thirty-five or so. A high birth rate is necessary to balance the many deaths. Populations grow slowly, if at all.

In stage two, the balance between death and birth rates ends. For one reason or another, death rates drop. More children survive, and people live healthier, longer lives. But births continue at high rates because for centuries people have believed that they *had* to have many children. These ideas are not given up quickly, so the result is a population "explosion."

Finally, in stage three, birth rates decline. People realize that fewer births are needed in order to have a certain family size, so they have fewer children and population growth slows.

Today, developing nations are in stage two of demographic transition. Death rates have fallen, but birth rates continue at high levels. However, the situation varies from nation to nation (and within nations, as with Kerala in India). The populations of Taiwan, Chile, Colombia, West Malaysia, and

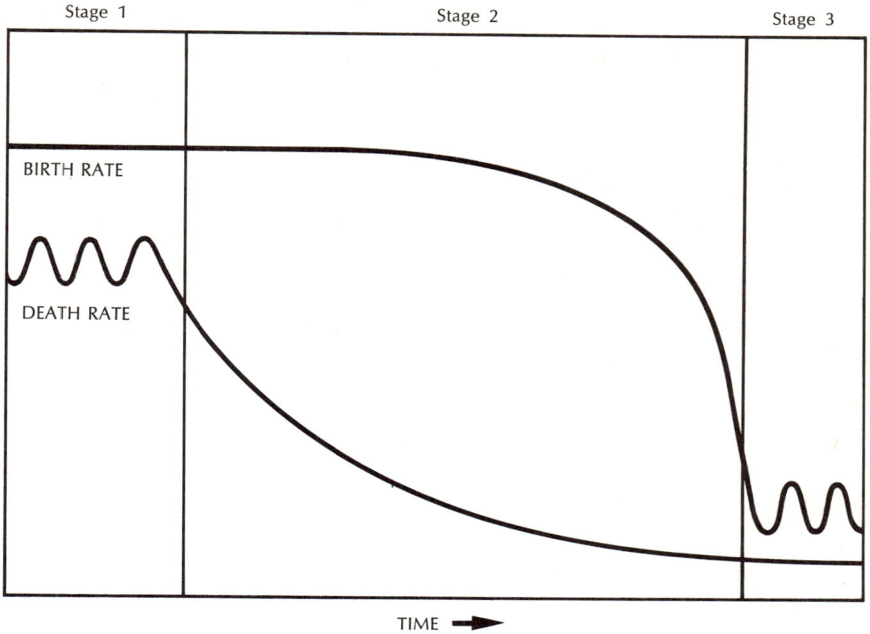


DEMOGRAPHIC TRANSITION

Sri Lanka (formerly Ceylon) seem headed for stage three. A decline in birth rates has clearly begun in these countries. The same is probably true of China, though little information is available about its population.

The demographic transition of nineteenth-century Europe has been the main model studied by population scientists. But questions have been raised about the causes of the population changes there. At one time, it was thought that the Industrial Revolution was largely responsible. It brought higher incomes and better education and health care, and caused many people to move from the country to cities. Studies have shown, however, that birth rates in parts of France began to drop *before* industrialization. It seems that demographic transition is more complex and less well understood than we once thought.

There are many differences between conditions in nineteenth-century Europe and today's developing nations. Death rates have dropped much more, and birth rates have risen much more swiftly than in Europe. And there is no great industrial development in today's developing nations to provide millions of rural people with jobs.

On the other hand, social change can occur more quickly nowadays. Modern birth-control methods are available, once people decide to make use of them. And other governments and international organizations such as the United Nations give encouragement and assistance. Factors like these may make fast demographic transitions possible. In industrialized nations the transition took between fifty and a hundred years. The same process may take only twenty to thirty years in developing nations today.

Peruvian mothers are taught child care by a representative of the Food and Agricultural Organization.

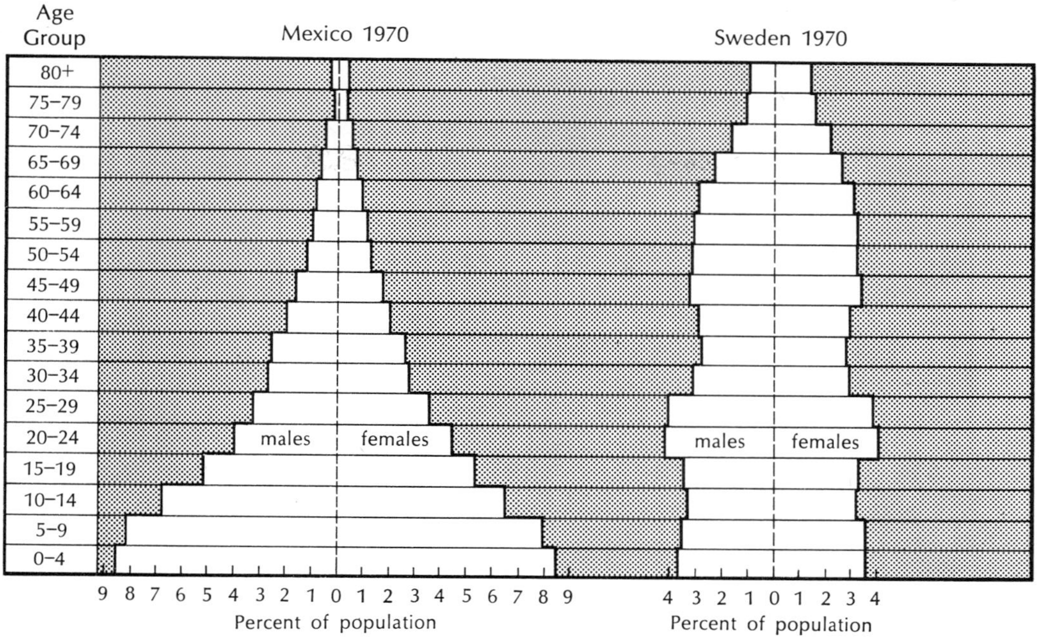


POPULATION PYRAMIDS

How can a nation such as India be helped toward demographic transition? What changes can convince people to have fewer children? Rapid industrialization is out of the question. Improved health care and birth-control devices are already available, but have had little effect on birth rates.

According to Dr. Harold Taylor of the Population Council, "A basic dictum is that parents will not stop having children until they believe that those they already have are going to survive." Although death rates in India have dropped, many infants and children still die. All over the earth, child death rates are highest where malnutrition is worst. Food, then, is the main key to further reductions in infant and child death rates—and to eventually lowering birth rates. Or as one scientist put it, "The best birth-control program is simply to feed the children."

Even if birth rates drop quickly, there will be practically

no effect on the world food situation for several years. The people who will eat most of the food grown in 1985 have already been born. It will take a long time for the world to reach zero population growth, when just enough children are born to replace people who die.

The United Nations has made three projections of population for the year 2000—6 billion, 6.5 billion, or 7.1 billion. UN demographers believe the middle figure is the one most likely to be reached. If these populations are projected beyond the year 2000, the most optimistic figures show the earth's population leveling off at 10 billion about the year 2100. The middle projection levels off with a population of 12.3 billion by 2125. The high projection is 16 billion people by the year 2135.

Many people doubt that these numbers will be reached, simply because the earth's resources and its people will not be able to stand the ecological, economic, and social stress. In his book *In the Human Interest,* Lester R. Brown wrote: "Population pressure will aggravate problems such as inflation, energy, food scarcity, and pollution. In the developing world, rural unemployment is rising to alarming levels, generating a massive movement of people from the countryside to cities unprepared for them."

Brown has proposed a plan for "putting on the demographic brakes." He believes that all of the developed nations can reach population stability by 1985. Along with sharp drops in birth rates of developing nations, this would cut world population growth to 1.1 percent per year in 1985. Brown envisions zero population growth by 2015, with a population of 6 billion.

Even if this goal is reached, Brown warns that there will still be extraordinary problems to deal with. India, struggling to feed almost 600 million people in 1975, would have nearly a billion by 2015. Mexico's population would grow from 55 to 103 million in the same period.

Many demographers and economists doubt that Lester Brown's timetable for reaching zero population growth can be achieved. He admits it is not an easy target. It depends on rapid, sweeping changes in human attitudes and behavior. And the changes will not happen without extraordinary aid from developed nations, aimed at helping developing nations to feed themselves.

# CHAPTER FOUR

# The Green Revolution

In *Gulliver's Travels*, Jonathan Swift wrote: "Whoever could make two ears of corn or two blades of grass to grow upon a spot of ground where only one grew before, would deserve better of mankind, and do more essential service to his country, than the whole race of politicians put together."

Our thanks, then, to plant breeders and others whose work has greatly increased food production. Through their efforts, U.S. food output per acre doubled over a span of forty years. Beginning in the mid-1940s, a few plant breeders and agronomists (scientists who study soils and crops) focused their attention on improving crop yields in the rest of the world. Their work resulted in extraordinary crops of wheat in Mexico, India, and other developing nations.

The adoption by developing nations of new high-yield varieties of grain was called the Green Revolution. The very

---

Dr. Norman E. Borlaug won the 1970 Nobel Peace Prize for his research on high-yield varieties of wheat.

name expresses the high hopes placed in this agricultural development. In 1970, Lester Brown wrote enthusiastically about the Green Revolution in his book *Seeds of Change*, but he also warned that there was a long list of "difficult, complex, sticky, second generation problems to face." He was right. The problems still exist, and have yet to be squarely faced.

The Green Revolution had a small beginning. In 1943, Mexico faced famine and asked the United States for help. The Rockefeller Foundation responded and set up a research center to improve Mexico's food production. One of the team of scientists at the center was Dr. Norman E. Borlaug, who was assigned the job of boosting wheat production.

At that time, Mexico's wheat yields were dismally low—sometimes only one-tenth the yield of an equal area of land in the United States. When fields were fertilized, the Mexican wheat plants grew top-heavy, fell over, and went to waste. They were also vulnerable to fungus diseases.

Dr. Borlaug believed that solutions to these and other problems lay in selective breeding. This is a painstaking process of crossbreeding different varieties of one species in order to get plants which combine the best characteristics of their "parents." When a dwarf wheat variety from Japan was crossed with other wheats at the Mexican research center, new varieties of short wheat resulted. They did not fall over when grown in fertilized fields. By the mid-1950s, researchers at the International Maize and Wheat Improvement Center, as it came to be called, had made dramatic progress in developing wheat plants suited to conditions in Mexico.

For a time, Mexico became a wheat-exporting nation.

Farmers in other developing nations began trying the new high-yield wheats. In 1960, the Rockefeller Foundation and the Ford Foundation joined forces to establish the International Rice Research Institute in the Philippines. A team of scientists there gathered 10,000 varieties of rice from all over the world and began crossbreeding. They soon produced a rice (called IR-8) that was capable of doubling the yields of most local Asian rices.

Use of the "miracle" grains, especially wheat, spread with extraordinary speed. In 1965, only 200 acres in Asia and North Africa were planted with the high-yield varieties. By 1973, about 80,200,000 acres were planted.

India had early success with the Green Revolution. Wheat output more than doubled in just seven years (1965–1972). By 1973, nearly 75 percent of India's wheat came from the new varieties. The Indian government predicted that the nation would soon become a wheat exporter. However, its

A biochemist in India analyzes the nutritional quality of bean seeds.

rich harvests were partly the result of favorable weather. When drought struck, the optimism began to disappear.

The picture grew darker as the costs of fuel and fertilizer rose. High-yield grains produce best when fertilized with nitrogen and watered by irrigation. During 1973–1974, fuel and fertilizer prices rose beyond the reach of many farmers in India and other developing nations. According to the U.S. Department of Agriculture, the lack of fuels and fertilizer was the main reason that India's wheat harvest was 23 million metric tons in 1974, rather than an expected 30 million metric tons.

As other problems emerged, critics spoke of "shattered dreams" and "disaster." But the Green Revolution was not a disaster. It had been oversold, especially by journalists and other writers. Even with its difficulties, it remained the earth's best chance to keep pace—for a while—with population growth.

The new varieties of plants themselves were the source of some early problems, Take the "miracle" rice IR-8, for example. Many rice eaters, it was discovered, didn't like its taste. They preferred, and paid more for, the native grains they were used to. Moreover, this new variety was unable to resist most of the diseases and pests which attack rice—leafhoppers, stem-borers, blight, blast, tungro virus, and grassy stunt. If the crops were not protected by insecticides and fungicides, severe crop losses were likely. If farmers could not afford these chemicals, or if they simply were not available, the pests frequently harvested the crop.

---

At a research station in India, a high-yield variety of rice is compared with a normal variety.

Use of the chemicals also brought problems. In Indonesia, farmers found that insecticides killed the fish in irrigation canals, as well as stem-borers and other insects. These fish were an important source of protein for Indonesian peasants.

All of the new high-yield varieties are more susceptible to pests because of the way they are grown. They are planted close together. Often there is multiple cropping—more than one crop a year. The dwarf rice plants have many leaves, and seem ideal living places for insects.

Of course the crop research centers are working to improve on their early efforts. In 1975, the International Rice Research Institute released three new strains of rice called IR-8, IR-29, and IR-30. All have strong or moderate resistance to most rice diseases and pests. All have improved taste and mature in 115 days or less, 45 days less than most varieties of rice in the tropics. Use of the new varieties should enable more farmers to grow multiple crops on their land.

Plant scientists are also working on varieties of rice that can survive under the extreme opposite conditions—flooded lowlands. Dwarf varieties do not do well in floods, which are increasingly common in several developing nations. A variety of fast-growing rice that keeps its top above water is being sought.

One of the most promising discoveries is a variety of corn called "opaque-2." Its kernels are white and opaque rather than yellow and translucent. It contains more than normal amounts of lysine, one of the essential amino acids. Widespread use of this corn would add vital protein to diets in areas where corn is a staple food.

However, "opaque-2" yields less grain per acre than other

Researchers use light boxes to separate protein-rich opaque corn kernels from normal kernels.

varieties. When ground up, it produces a finer flour than the traditional kinds of corn. People found that their favorite recipes for corn breads and other foods did not turn out right with the new flour, so they chose to stay with the old kinds of corn. Plant breeders have not given up on "opaque-2," though, and they expect to develop high-lysine corn that is acceptable to consumers.

Unfortunately, the greatest problems of the Green Revolution have little to do with protein content or pests. They

involve politics, economics, and ancient customs, and they won't be solved in laboratories or on experimental farms.

One of the greatest dangers of the Green Revolution is that it will increase unemployment in developing nations. History shows large-scale agricultural development can cause rural unemployment. This happened in the United States, where millions of people left their farms and moved to towns and cities. Usually they found jobs there. In the developing nations, there is a somewhat similar shift of population to cities, although roughly 70 percent of the people still live in rural areas. But the limited industrial development thus far in the developing nations cannot provide jobs for the growing millions of jobless people. It makes sense, therefore, to keep as many people as possible "down on the farm." Critics of the Green Revolution fear that it is having the opposite effect, and there is some evidence to support their claims.

Since the high-yield plants require fertilizers, irrigation, and often insecticides, they are first used by farmers who can afford these extras. A peasant with only a few acres of land may not even be able to borrow the money needed for the new seeds and chemicals. So the new varieties are planted mostly by those who own the most land, and these farmers get richer. The Green Revolution may be widening the gap between the rich and the poor.

Also, many peasants have no land at all. They live as tenant farmers on large farms. In some places the tenant farmers have been evicted because the land on which they live has become more valuable as cropland. Peasants are also losing jobs because they are being replaced by machines. The Green Revolution has given the people with the larger farms enough profit so they can afford to buy tractors and mechanical

reapers. According to one estimate, by 1984 nearly 20 percent of the farm labor in the Punjab state of India will be replaced by machines.

Actually, the Green Revolution has the potential for providing many rural jobs. The high-yield varieties require more work in soil preparation, planting, weeding, and harvesting. Since high-yield plants mature faster than other plants, in some places two crops are possible in a growing season. This doubles the need for labor. In the long run, however, these positive effects may be overcome by machines. It may become necessary for governments to encourage the use of more human labor on farms, for example, by putting high import taxes on tractors and other farm machinery.

The Green Revolution can also have powerful effects on long-established social, political, and economic customs. It can upset the status quo, and some people don't want that to

happen. Consider what occurred in Java when the government launched a program to increase rice production. Farmers were offered low-interest loans to buy new seeds and chemicals. It seemed an ideal plan, but it was doomed because of traditional economic and political factors in Javanese villages.

Most village farmers in Java own plots of less than an acre, too small to support their families. They need outside jobs, but such jobs are scarce. Most of them are forced to borrow from the wealthy people of the village—large landowners, town employees, and government officials. In return, they agree to work for the wealthy people whenever necessary. In effect, they are permanently in debt, with no chance to become independent.

The high-yield seeds of the Green Revolution threatened to change this situation. So, those in power made sure that the poorest peasants did not take advantage of the government program. News of the low-cost loans was kept secret; wealthy patrons discouraged peasants from trying the new seeds. As a result, few peasants took the risk. The government assistance was used mostly by the rich, who became richer. In south-central Java, some wealthy people began buying land from poor families, sending more jobless people to city slums. And wealthy farmers began buying rice-field tractors, eliminating more rural jobs. Summing up the situation, anthropologist Richard W. Franke said, "The Green Revolution in Java offers only the choice between servitude and homelessness."

The developers of the high-yield plants want peasants to take advantage of the new varieties. In fact, Dr. Norman Borlaug has said, "If we can't get the Green Revolution to the little guy, there is no revolution."

This isn't likely to happen unless there are effective national programs to inform farmers and to provide them with low-cost loans and other help. Dr. Borlaug has said, "Our primary concern has to be to produce food. We're not a land-reform agency. Governments are just going to have to find some way to give these people seed and fertilizer and water—outright."

One of the Green Revolution's severest critics is Dr. Marvin Harris, an anthropologist at Columbia University. He has called high-yield seeds "antimiracles." He writes: "The so-called miracle seeds are only more productive if they are planted in conjunction with optimum levels of irrigation water, chemical fertilizers, and pesticides. A true miracle seed, designed to meet the existing conditions of peasant

The "little guy" is the key to success of the Green Revolution.

agriculture, would have different specifications, since 70 to 90 percent of Asian farm families have no irrigation water and no cash or credit for the purchase of chemical products."

Defenders of the Green Revolution argue that even without fertilizer, the high-yield seeds produce more than the old varieties. And they say that those who are most negative about the Green Revolution know the least about it.

Still, the very idea of transplanting American agricultural practices abroad can be questioned. Energy shortages and rising fuel costs during the 1970s awakened us all to the fact that American agriculture uses a lot of energy. Does it make sense to encourage millions of poor farmers to depend on fossil fuels, which are fast being used up and are bound to become more costly? No, it doesn't make much sense, but there doesn't seem to be any alternative, and the earth's population increases by 80 million people each year.

It is too early to judge the full effects of the Green Revolution. It took farmers in the United States one or two decades before they fully adopted high-yield corn. The governments and farmers of developing countries will also need time in order to deal with the opportunities and problems offered them by the new seeds.

Meanwhile, the scientists at research centers have their work cut out for them. One goal is to breed new varieties of plants that are more resistant to pests and diseases. But even when resistance is achieved, success is short-lived. A new variety of pest soon evolves, and is able to attack the formerly resistant plants.

A Mexican plant breeder explained the challenge of maintaining wheat resistance to fungus diseases called rusts: "One variety of wheat may survive about four or five years before the fungus mutates into a new virulent strain. Every year we collect all the rust we can find in Mexico. We can tell when a new rust is emerging, and we know then that it is time to switch to a new wheat. Other scientists are doing the same in other countries.

"This process will never end, but at least we think we can keep ahead of the rust. A new mutant doesn't cause an epidemic right away; its numbers are too small. It must spread and multiply before it can cause much trouble. By that time, after several years, we are ready with a new wheat."

Being well-prepared to deal with plant pests and diseases is vitally important. In 1970, 15 percent of the U.S. corn crop—some 700 million bushels—was destroyed by a new mutant strain of blight. It was damaging to just one variety of corn, but that type was grown on almost every farm in America. Fortunately the United States was able to switch to a blight-resistant corn variety the following year.

Less developed countries may not be able to respond so quickly to the appearance of a new pest variety. They need to have their own plant-breeding centers. At such centers, new varieties of plants can be tested against local diseases, and more resistance bred into them if necessary. (The centers can also give the new varieties local names; this makes the seeds more acceptable to farmers.)

The 1970 corn blight in the United States drew attention to the dangers of monocrop (one crop) farming. Normally a great variety of food plants are grown in developing nations. Indonesia has 600 different kinds of rice; Bangladesh has 1,200 varieties. In contrast, just 2 varieties of peas make up 95 percent of the entire crop in the United States. This country's crops of sugar beets, wheat, beans, corn, and sor-

The effects of corn leaf blight and wheat leaf rust illustrate the need for improved pest resistance in food plants.

ghum are also quite uniform. This is the sort of agriculture that is at the heart of the Green Revolution. And monocrops of high-yield seeds increase the risk of major crop losses to diseases and pests.

As new high-yield varieties of grains are adopted in developing nations, they replace native varieties. Many native varieties are dying out. This loss has been called a "genetic erosion." Each variety of plant (and animal) has a unique combination of genes which determine its characteristics. It is these genes which plant breeders combine and recombine in order to develop plants with the characteristics they want. The more genetic variety they have to work with, the better.

Seed "banks" have been set up in order to stop genetic erosion. The largest corn bank, in Mexico, holds 12,000 varieties; the largest wheat bank is near Washington, D.C., and contains 23,000 varieties. Not nearly enough money is spent on such collections. And some seed banks have been lost through accidents or carelessness.

It is vitally important to save as much genetic variety as possible before more is lost. Genetic conservation is one concern of the plant-breeding centers of the Green Revolution. An International Board of Plant Genetic Resources has been established. Its goals are to encourage the development of seed banks, point out the most serious genetic erosion problems, and support collection efforts.

Other kinds of Green Revolution research centers have also been set up. In 1975, there were ten independent but cooperating centers, in the Philippines, Mexico, Nigeria, Colombia, India, Peru, Kenya, Ethiopia, and Liberia. Their budget grew from $15 million in 1972 to $48 million in 1975.

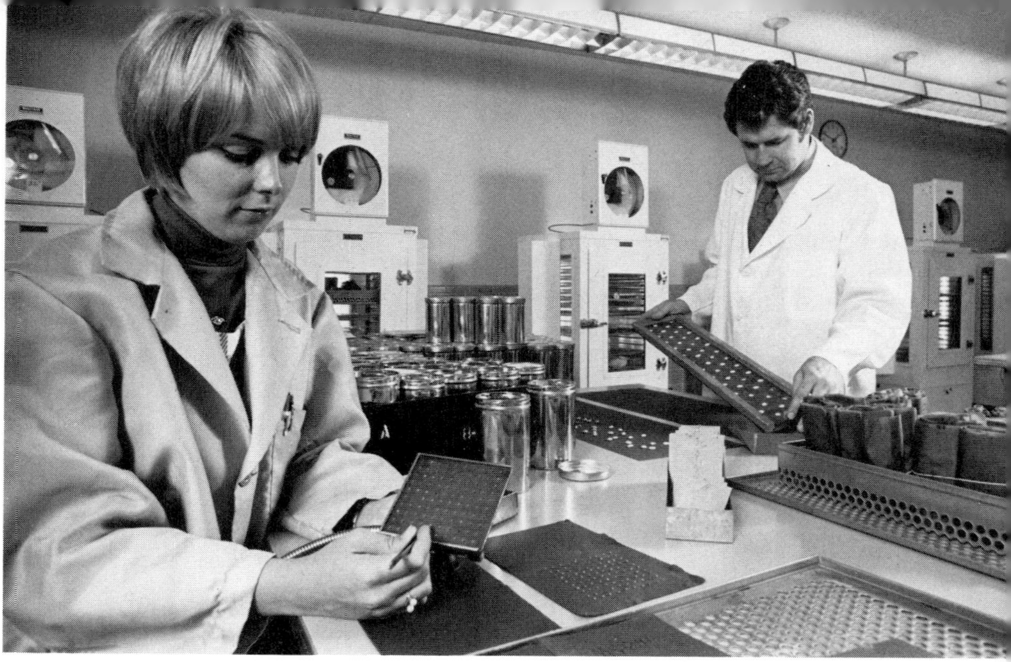

The viability of seeds is tested at the National Seed Storage Laboratory in Fort Collins, Colorado.

This network may be joined by the Asian Vegetable Research and Development Center in Taiwan. Some projects at these centers include: developing a rice drier which is fueled with discarded rice hulls rather than oil; improving yields of such crops as cassava, cowpeas, field beans, millet, and pigeon peas (an important crop in India); and improving disease resistance in cattle, potatoes, rice, and wheat.

Another goal is to improve the protein content of grains. Work continues on high-lysine corn (such as "opaque-2"). In Ethiopia, two varieties of sorghum were found which have twice the lysine of the kinds usually grown. These high-lysine varieties have been grown for centuries by Ethiopian farmers because of their pleasing flavor. However, they produce less grain per acre than other kinds of sorghum. Plant breeders are trying to develop varieties of sorghum which combine high lysine content with high yield. Success would be an important development for the arid

regions of Africa and Asia, where sorghum is a basic food for about 300 million people.

Some progress has been made at improving the protein content of rice. The importance of this cannot be overestimated. According to the International Rice Research Institute, about 1.3 billion people get more than half of their food energy from rice.

The International Maize and Wheat Improvement Center of Mexico has had many successes, but perhaps none as potentially great as the creation of an entirely new kind of grain, called triticale (pronounced *trit-i-kaley*). It is a cross between wheat and rye. Triticale has the high-yield characteristics of wheat and the drought and disease resistance of rye. It surpasses wheat in both total protein and lysine content.

Triticale may do especially well in semiarid regions, such as the Sahel of Africa. There are already hundreds of thousands of acres planted to triticale in the United States. It is used mostly for livestock food but also for such products as triticakes and tritipizza.

Other possibilities in plant breeding may require many years of research. With fertilizer costs rising, scientists are especially interested in improving the self-fertilizing ability of plants. Certain plants called legumes (peas, beans, alfalfa, and clover, to name a few) are able to take nitrogen gas from the air and change it into solid nitrogen compounds. Nitrogen in this form can then be used by the legumes or by other plants nearby.

---

By injecting bacteria into individual corn plants, scientists are able to determine which plants are most resistant to stalk rot.

Such legumes as red clover (above) and crown vetch are often planted to help restore nitrogen to soils.

The nitrogen-making process (called nitrogen-fixing) is made possible by bacteria that live within the legume roots. Tropical grasses, including sugar cane, are able to do the same with the aid of bacteria that live in their roots or in the soil around them.

Scientists are studying the relationships between nitrogen-fixing bacteria and plants. They hope to be able to stimulate production of this natural source of nitrogen fertilizer. Plant breeders also hope to produce other plants such as wheat which will have the nitrogen-fixing ability of legumes. A few years ago such a development might have been called impossible. New methods of plant breeding now make it seem more reasonable.

In 1975, Brazilian scientists reported that one kind of nitrogen-fixing bacteria (called *Spirillum lipoferum*) can live in corn roots. Some produced very little nitrogen, but others fixed nitrogen almost as well as the bacteria in soybeans, a legume. The *Spirillum* bacteria seems to work best in the tropics, but scientists are investigating its use in colder areas. To develop self-fertilizing food plants would surely be an accomplishment worthy of the name "Green Revolution."

There are good reasons to worry about the future effects of the Green Revolution. It has already intensified some social problems and has the potential of causing even more disturbing changes, all the way from village life to the national and international level. Yet with all of its real and potential problems, the Green Revolution seems to be our only hope of increasing food output at a pace near that of our population growth.

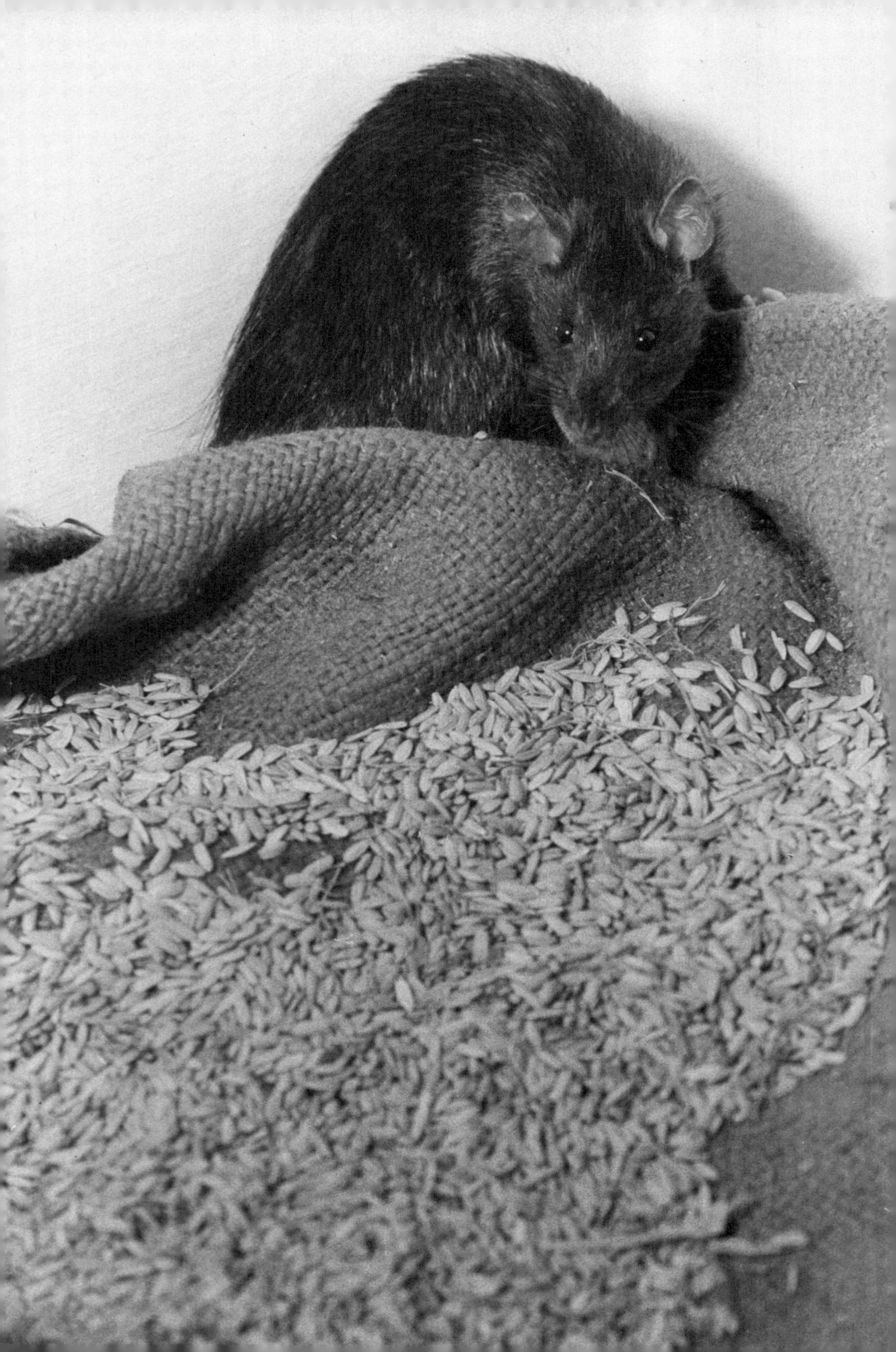

CHAPTER FIVE

# The Good News and the Bad News

During most of the 1960s and 1970s, food production grew faster than population. Some food experts expect this to continue for many years. They foresee possibilities for great increases in food output. Others are less hopeful, and worry about the costs, to people and the environment, of rapid agricultural development.

A logical first step toward providing more food is simply to protect food that is already grown. No one knows the total amount of food lost to pests, but experts agree that it is a huge loss. Perhaps 30 percent of annual food production is eaten, destroyed, or otherwise damaged by insects, rodents, molds, bacteria, viruses, weeds, and other pests. The losses occur in fields, during shipment, and in storage. Pests represent only a small fraction of all living things, but they do tremendous damage.

In Africa and Asia, a grain-eating bird called the quelea causes serious losses of rice, wheat, and other grains. Queleas

Rats eat grain that could save the lives of people.

daily eat an estimated 300 tons of grain in the Sudan area alone. In central Africa, the tsetse fly spreads a disease called sleeping sickness among cattle, and prevents cattle-raising on more than four million acres of grazing land.

Reduced losses to pests will bring an immediate increase in food available to people. The greatest gains can be made by protecting food during storage. Stored food is poorly protected in many developing nations. An estimated 90 percent of the grain grown in India is not stored safely. We already know *how* to solve most pest problems in stored foods. If the governments of developing countries act to improve storage facilities, millions of tons of food will be saved.

Pest control in fields can also be improved. Plant breeders have already had some success in developing plants that resist pest attacks. This resistance is usually lost within five to fifteen years, however, so there is a constant challenge to develop new resistant varieties. Pest problems can also be

Worldwide, inadequate protection of grain (left) results in more food loss than outbreaks of locusts (above).

reduced by changes in the time of planting and the methods and time of harvest.

The natural enemies of pests can be used to reduce pest numbers. Among the most successful are little wasps which lay their eggs on the bodies or eggs of plant-eating insects. After a wasp larva hatches, it feeds on the pest and kills it. Several kinds of insect pests have been brought under control this way. Unfortunately, methods like these usually require expensive, time-consuming research, which few developing nations seem able to support.

Perhaps the worst news about pest control is that, for the foreseeable future, the main remedy will be chemical poisons (biocides). They are already used, and misused, all over the world. Agriculture in the United States depends heavily on biocides, yet our crop losses have increased. Several

insect pests have evolved resistance to biocides that once were effective.

Some biocides have been outlawed in the United States because they had bad effects on the environment and were judged to be threats to human health. Besides DDT, the

biocides aldrin, dieldrin, chlordane, and heptachor are suspected of causing cancer in humans. Use of these biocides has been (or will be) banned in the United States, yet it is legal to export them to developing nations. In these countries, as in the United States, most farmers get advice on pest control, either directly or indirectly, from biocide manufacturers. Their main concern is selling a product, even though there is plenty of evidence that biocides often make pest problems worse. Since most farmers in developing countries are not well-educated, there is good reason to fear that biocides will be misused even more than they are in America.

Development of crop land in the Amazon Basin will be difficult and expensive.

Besides trying to reduce food losses, there are several ways in which we might try to increase food production. For example, what about increasing the amount of farmland? Seventy percent of the earth's land is too dry, too cold, or otherwise unsuitable to support crops. There are about 7 billion acres of land used for grazing. Only about 3.6 billion acres are now cultivated. That's less than an acre per person.

Some people say that the amount of arable land can be more than doubled. Much of this potential farmland is in such tropical areas as central Africa and the Amazon Basin of Brazil. Of course, there are usually good reasons why much of this potentially usable land is not being cultivated. In West Africa, for example, some 16 million acres of fertile river-valley land are not farmed because black flies there spread "river blindness," a disease which affects a million Africans. This land will remain idle unless the flies are brought under control.

It is easy to talk about doubling the amount of arable land, but doing it is another matter. Lester Brown has said, "The people who are talking about adding more land are not considering the cost. If you are willing to pay the price, you can farm the slopes of Mt. Everest."

Efforts to grow more food have already damaged some existing arable acres, and threaten to ruin more. During 1974, nearly 9 million acres of unfarmed land were put into production in the United States. Part of this was natural grassland, part was forest, but most was former farmland that had been left idle. According to the Soil Conservation Service, less than half of this new farmland had adequate protection against soil erosion. As a result, an estimated 60

Overgrazing and other land abuse leads to erosion in Kentucky (above) and India (right).

million tons of topsoil—the most fertile soil layer—is lost from such land each year.

This is serious, but it seems mild compared with the damage done to land in Asia, the Middle East, and Africa. The Sahel area of Africa is just one region where once-fertile land is becoming desert. In India, large parts of the state of Rajasthan were once wooded, while other parts supported livestock and crops. As numbers of people and livestock have grown, trees have been cut down and grasses overgrazed. Much of the topsoil is blowing away. Each year about 30,000 acres of this state become a man-made desert.

Stripping land of its trees and other plant cover not only speeds soil erosion by wind and water, but also helps create bigger and more frequent floods. Forests in the foothills of the Himalayas are fast disappearing. As a result, floods are getting worse in South Asia. A 1973 flood in Pakistan destroyed large amounts of stored grain. And in 1974, floods in Bangladesh and India damaged crops almost as much as drought.

In more developed nations such as the United States, much farmland is lost when highways, industries, and homes are built. Worldwide, some efforts are being made to stop loss of cropland. But prospects for large-scale increase in the amount of arable land seem dim. It appears that we will have to make do with what we have now.

To produce more food, then, we must grow more on the land we have. In 1909, an American farmer could expect

to harvest just 26 bushels of corn per acre; by the mid-1970s he could expect 87 bushels per acre. There have been less dramatic rises with other crops. In seventy-five years the Japanese have managed to double their rice yields. There is an unknown upper limit to this, of course.

Developed nations may be reaching the upper limits of grain yields, but there is still room for improvement in many other countries. India has about the same farm acreage as the United States, but yields only two-fifths as much food. Corn yields in Brazil are less than a third of those in the United States, and rice yields in India and Nigeria are a third of those in Japan.

It is foolish to assume, however, that all nations can match the U.S. corn yield or the Japanese rice yield. Crop yields of different countries (and even of different farms), vary for several reasons, including type of soil, amount and timing of rainfall, temperature, amount of fertilizer used, and the differing abilities of farmers.

Wheat and rice yields in India have already dropped since the beginning of the Green Revolution. At first the high-yield varieties produced four times the grain of older varieties. At that time the new varieties were planted on India's best land. As the acreage planted with high-yield seeds increased and began to include poorer land, the average yield fell to two and a half times the yield of older varieties. So we should not expect high food output in one place to be duplicated everywhere else.

Most high-yield plants mature faster than older varieties, and this makes *multiple crops* possible, especially in the year-round warm climate near the equator. The idea of rais-

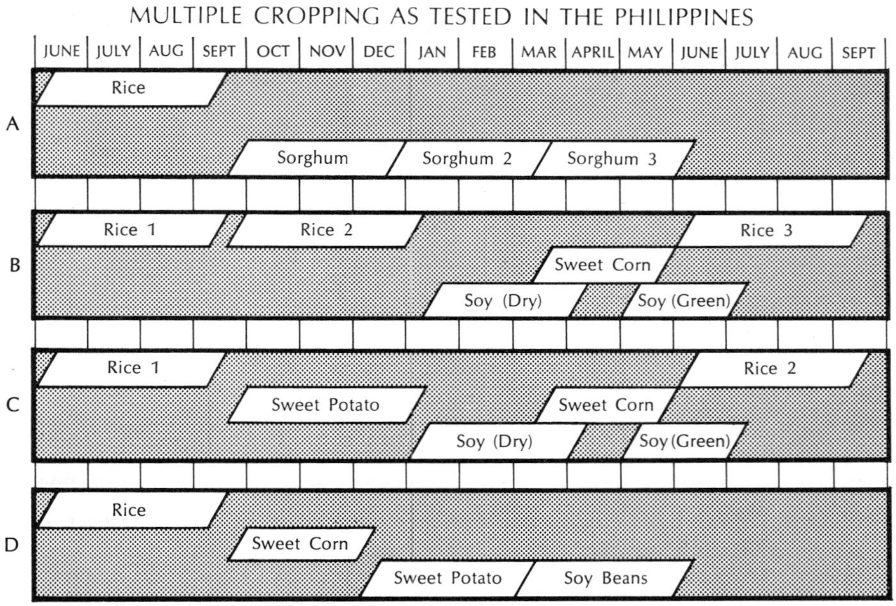


In a year's time, as many as five crops can be raised on plots of land in the tropics.

ing more than one crop a year is not new; it has been practiced for at least 6,000 years. In southern China, three grain crops are often grown on the same plot of land each year.

*Intercropping*—two or more crops grown at the same time—is common in northern China. Generally, wheat is planted first; then corn is planted between the wheat rows. The wheat matures and is harvested before the corn is high enough to overshadow it. The corn matures about two months later.

Multiple crops are grown on about half of China's farmland. All of Taiwan's arable land yields an average of two crops a year. In contrast, only about 18 percent of India's farmland is multicropped. Opportunities for multicropping are being investigated at field stations of the Indian Agricultural Research Institute.

Increased use of multicropping can add millions of tons of grain to world food output. It can also create more rural jobs. Of course, multicropping has its own set of problems—depleting the soil of nutrients, increasing the problems of pest control, and often increasing the need for irrigation water.

The opposite of multicropping is a farming practice called fallowing, in which no crops are grown for a year or more. Leaving land idle, or fallow, is vital for maintaining soil fertility and moisture, especially in semiarid regions. More than 25 million acres of western wheat lands in the United States are usually left fallow each year. Fallowing is also common in Canada, Australia, and the Soviet Union. Even though fallowing takes land out of production temporarily,

Grain planted with young tobacco plants helps prevent wind erosion.

it is necessary if the soil is to keep producing good crops. This practice must become more widespread in developing nations if they are to halt the deterioration of their land.

Of all the factors which affect world food production, none is more important than water. High-yield varieties grow best on irrigated land and have been adopted in areas where irrigation is available.

Irrigation is especially vital wherever rainfall is spread unevenly through the year. Large parts of India and Pakistan get plenty of rain, but it falls mostly from June to September. For the rest of the year, the land is semiarid. Under these conditions, irrigation is the key to successful farming. Farmers in India, Pakistan, and other developing nations are eager for dependable water supplies.

Strips of fallow land are a common sight in wheat-raising areas of North Dakota.

The amount of irrigated land has grown tremendously in recent years. In 1950, 260 million acres were irrigated. Just twenty years later, 470 million acres were irrigated. More than a fourth of this land is in China.

The tremendous increase in the amount of irrigated land is not mainly a result of huge dams and networks of canals. Most of the increase is a result of individual farmers drilling water wells. In just six years, from 1965 to 1971, the number of private wells in India quadrupled. But this growth rate is not expected to continue. According to Lester Brown, the amount of irrigated land in the world will probably increase at barely 1 percent a year for the rest of this century.

While some land is being irrigated for the first time, other irrigated areas are being abandoned. Salts from irrigation water build up in the soil if fields are not properly drained. After centuries of irrigation, vast areas of Iraq are coated with these salts and are useless as farmland. India has lost 15 million acres of irrigated land in the same way. Solving this problem is difficult, costly, and time-consuming.

The expansion of irrigation may also be limited by underground water supplies. In parts of the southwestern United States, underground water supplies have been used faster than they were replenished by rainfall. Some irrigated farms have had to be abandoned.

In drip irrigation, a one-eighth-inch plastic hose carries water directly to plant roots.

A new kind of irrigation, developed in Israel, wastes much less water than older ways. Rows of pipes release water frequently and lightly onto the soil right near crop roots. Experiments have shown that this "trickle" or "drip" irrigation has many advantages over older methods. It produces crop yields equal to or better than other methods, yet uses only one-third to one-half as much water. It also washes less fertilizer out of the soil and reduces weed growth. One scientist went so far as to call trickle irrigation a "Blue Revolution."

The use of drip irrigation is growing rapidly and will help stretch water supplies. But the equipment needed for this type of irrigation is probably too expensive for developing nations. However, even in these countries the method may be modified so it can be used, perhaps by planting certain crops around small basins dug in the ground.

In the future, water supplies may be used more efficiently by the plants themselves. Plant breeders may be able to produce varieties of rice and other plants that need less water than normal. The kinds of rice planted now use huge amounts of water. If water becomes quite scarce in an area, rice may have to be phased out in favor of more water-efficient plants, such as wheat and sorghum.

Fertilizer is another important factor in the future of world food production. Its use has grown five times since 1950, and the resulting increase in food represents the meals of at least a billion people. Eighty million metric tons of chemical fertilizers were used in 1974; 110 million metric tons will be needed in 1980, in order to keep pace with the food needs of a growing population.

There are abundant supplies of the three main fertilizer nutrients—phosphate, potash, and nitrogen. Reserves of high-quality phosphate rock are expected to last for 450 to 600 years, and there are much greater amounts of lower-grade ore. Most of the potash made today comes from potassium chloride mined from ancient salt lake beds. Half of all fertilizer is manufactured from nitrogen, the most abundant gas in the air.

Fertilizer shortages have not been caused by a lack of resources, but by a lack of planning. The fertilizer industry has a history of "boom or bust." When fertilizer supplies ran short in the mid-1960s, the industry expanded and increased its output. Prices dropped, and expansion stopped. Then demand for fertilizers began to increase once more, but the industry was slow to respond. A severe shortage caused high prices in 1973, making it clear that many new fertilizer plants were needed. Ten new nitrogen fertilizer plants are planned for China alone, but world fertilizer production may not catch up with demand for many years.

Fertilizer will never be cheap again. Even when supplies become adequate, the cost of producing fertilizer will remain high and probably rise. Fertilizer production is complex and uses great amounts of energy. Although the nitrogen used in fertilizer comes from the air and is free, the process of "fixing" it chemically requires lots of natural gas or other fossil fuels, which are becoming more and more costly as the earth's resources are being depleted.

Most phosphate (below) and other fertilizer is used in developed nations, though it is needed for growing more food in developing nations (right).

When fertilizer is in short supply, all nations—rich and poor—compete for available reserves. The developing nations have limited funds, yet they often need fertilizer in order to produce a minimum diet for their people. In terms of world food production, the best place to use scarce fertilizer is in the developing nations. Levels of nitrogen, phosphate, and potash in their soils are so low that a pound of fertilizer stimulates the growth of at least ten pounds of grain. American and European fields, on the other hand, are already richly fertilized and produce only two to five pounds of grain from a pound of fertilizer.

Today, the developed nations use more than 80 percent of all fertilizer made. Some of the consequences are mind-boggling. A nation like India, for lack of a pound of fertilizer costing fifteen cents, fails to grow ten pounds of grain which she must then import at a cost of a dollar or more. The population of India is nearly three times that of the United States, yet Indian agriculture struggles along with three million tons of fertilizer a year. In the United States, the same amount of fertilizer is used on gardens, golf courses, and lawns of homes and cemeteries.

With all of the benefits of using fertilizers, their use can cause special problems. For example, pest problems are sometimes worse in fertilized fields than in unfertilized ones. Also, crop plants usually recover only 50 percent of the nitrogen and 30 percent of the phosphate for each application of fertilizer. If fertilizer was used more completely by plants, less would be needed.

One solution to this problem may be a sort of "timed-release" fertilizer, such as urea coated with sulphur. Urea is a white compound made from ammonia and carbon dioxide. It is about half nitrogen and is fast becoming the most widely used nitrogen fertilizer in Asia. A coating of sulphur on pellets of urea allows the nitrogen to be released slowly. Only one application is needed for each crop. Field trials show that the gradual release of nitrogen enables rice plants to use more of it.

Unused fertilizer washes out of the soil and into underground water supplies or into streams, ponds, and lakes. In water, as on land, fertilizer stimulates plant growth. Up to a point, this is fine. However, many lakes and ponds, especially in developed nations, have become overfertilized (eutrophic). Great growths of algae and other water plants choke the shallows. As plants die and decay, they use up oxygen. Declining oxygen content in the water causes fish and other animals to die, with the more desirable food-fish usually dying first. The increased use of fertilizers in developing nations will inevitably lead to similar water-pollution problems.

In the long run, a dependence on commercial fertilizers may cause even more serious problems. We don't know much about the long-term effects of heavy fertilizer use, but there are some disturbing bits of evidence. Recent samples of well water from heavily fertilized areas of Ohio and Illinois contain concentrations of nitrates that can cause birth defects and infant deaths. This discovery may be a warning that water supplies under large regions could become polluted, thus endangering human health.

Concern about the long-term effects of commercial fertilizers, along with their rising costs, has prompted some scientists to look for alternatives. One method once widely used is to plant a legume like clover every two or three years. A clover crop can add 150 pounds of nitrogen per acre (more than is normally applied). A legume called winter vetch can be planted in corn fields in late summer and then plowed under in the spring, thus providing the soil with 133 pounds of nitrogen per acre.

Manure and other wastes, including human body wastes, are also being investigated as sources of nutrients for crops. Manure has several advantages over commercial fertilizers. It improves the soil's water-holding capacity, reduces erosion, and adds beneficial bacteria and fungi. A year's manure from one dairy cow, nine hogs, or eighty-four chickens yields as much fertilizer as farmers usually apply to an acre of corn in the United States.

There's plenty of manure available—an estimated 1.7

billion tons in the United States along. A lot of it is concentrated in feed lots, where great numbers of livestock are fattened before slaughter. However, given the cost of transporting and spreading manure, most farmers prefer commercial fertilizers, which are also easier to use. Rising costs of commercial fertilizers will probably stimulate more interest in manure and other wastes, including crop leftovers, garbage, and sewage. In China, human body wastes have been used as fertilizer for centuries. However, disease problems caused by this "night soil," as it is called, have not yet been solved.

A small but growing number of farmers in the United States has stopped using commercial fertilizers and bio-

Manure is plentiful in cattle feedlots but cannot be transported long distances economically.

cides completely. Their so-called "organic" farms usually produce smaller yields than other farms, but are profitable because such farmers have fewer expenses. Some people believe that organic farming might become a large-scale alternative to the kind of farming practiced today.

Organic farming methods have been studied very little by agricultural scientists. For many years nearly all of the research money and effort has gone to the kind of farming that uses lots of fossil fuels, biocides, and commercial fertilizers. A long-term study comparing the two ways of farming is being conducted by the Center for the Biology of Natural Systems, at Washington University in St. Louis.

There is one more factor affecting world food production, but that is something over which we have no control—the weather. Recent history has shown that weather changes can turn optimistic crop forecasts into gloomy harvests. With world food reserves low, there is growing concern about the weather and about possible changes in global weather patterns.

In the mid-1970s, some meteorologists (weather scientists) said that a pattern of North American drought could be traced back to the time of the Civil War. According to these scientists, drought strikes North America about every twenty years. The last severe drought occurred in the mid-1930s; it was followed by a mild one in the mid-1950s. On the basis of this theory, some meteorologists predicted another drought would occur during the 1970s. Other meteorologists disagreed with this theory, saying that weather varies at random, following no regular pattern. The study of climate changes is a new one, and full of uncertainty.

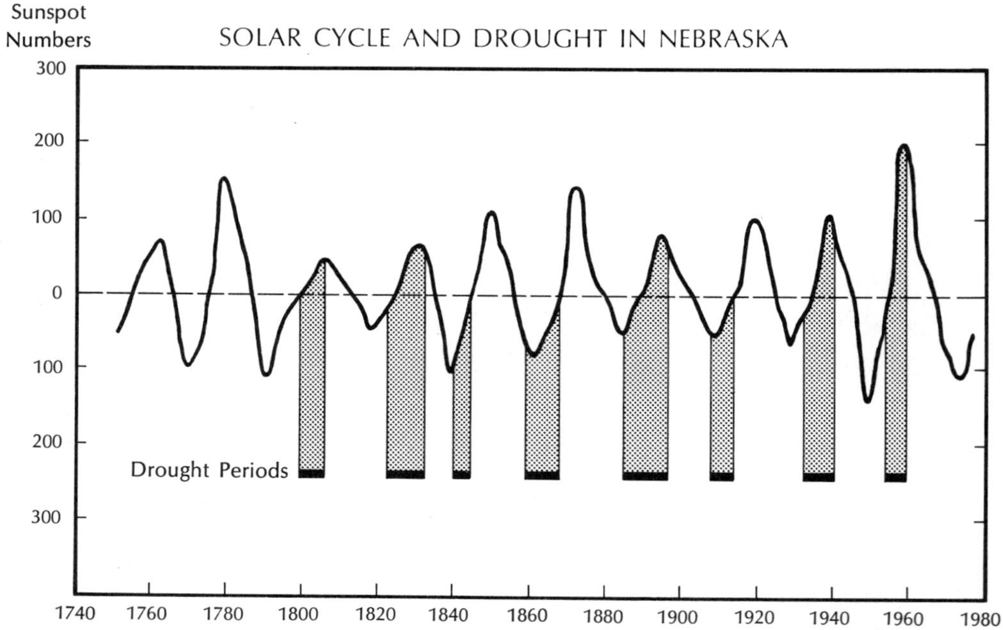


The earth's weather patterns may be affected by changes in activity of sunspots, which are strong magnetic forces on the sun. Weather data seems to show that droughts have occurred in Nebraska about every twenty years.

Other controversial weather theories have been suggested. For example, there is evidence that human activities are affecting the world's weather. Pollution from industries, automobiles, and land abuse in semiarid regions has increased the number of dust particles in the atmosphere. This reduces the amount of sunlight reaching the earth's surface. As a result, the temperature of the earth has been getting slightly cooler since about 1940.

According to some meteorologists, the greatest cooling has taken place in the polar regions. Cold polar air in the Northern Hemisphere is pushing farther south, deflecting the northern movement of monsoon rains. If this theory is correct, it explains the recent severe Sahelian drought. And it leads meteorologists to expect years of low rainfall in India and Southeast Asia.

In the early 1900s, severe droughts hit northern India frequently, every three or four years. Then the monsoon rains shifted northward, and drought became less common. A southward shift of the monsoon rains may bring back drought conditions like those early in the century.

The world's weather has been the subject of several recent conferences, studies, and reports. A 1974 workshop sponsored by the International Federation of Institutes of Advanced Study came to some grim conclusions. The scientists said that a new pattern of global weather was emerging, and that climates would be more variable than in recent decades. The scientists concluded: "We believe that this climatic change poses a threat to the people of the world. The direction of climate change indicates major crop failures almost certainly within the decade. This, coinciding with a period of almost nonexistent grain reserves, can be ignored only at the risk of great suffering and mass starvation."

No wonder that many people, not just meteorologists, are keeping a close watch on the world's weather.

## CHAPTER SIX

# Beyond "Clean Your Plate"

For decades, people have sought new sources of food—to find new tastes, to gain better nutrition, and simply to feed everyond on earth. Protein foods are especially sought after.

Seafood is rich in protein, and people used to believe that we could count on "the unlimited riches of the seas" to feed billions of people. Between 1950 and 1970, many nations invested in modern fishing fleets. As a result, the world fish catch rose dramatically, from 21 million metric tons to 70 million metric tons. Some people expected the catch to keep rising. Instead, it declined for several years. It may eventually reach 100 million metric tons, but now the main concern is sustaining the present level and protecting overfished species from extinction.

The California sardine has been nearly wiped out. Now protected by law, it may increase enough by the year 2000 to be fished again. New England haddock are also so scarce that commercial fishermen are forbidden to seek them anywhere off eastern North America. Herring have almost

disappeared from the North Sea and the coast of Europe. Some kinds of tuna, salmon, and cod have also been overfished. And several species of whale (mammals, not fish) have been hunted to near extinction.

One of the most spectacular examples of overfishing occurred off the coast of Peru. In the early 1960s, Peru accounted for a fifth of the total world catch. It harvested millions of tons of anchovies, which were then processed into fish meal (mostly used in poultry and pig feed). In 1972 the anchovies became scarce. At first their disappearance was blamed entirely on a shift of the Humboldt Current off Peru. But a study by marine biologists put most of the blame on several years of overfishing which prevented the anchovies from reproducing their numbers.

In order for a population of fish (or of any other animal) to maintain itself, a certain number must be left for breeding. Present catches of many kinds of popular food-fishes do not allow them to sustain their numbers. As long as this situation continues, the world fish catch may drop even lower. Meanwhile, competition between fishing nations grows sharper. The basic idea seems to be "grab what you can and don't worry about tomorrow." Large fleets from Japan and the Soviet Union roam all over the world. Disputes flare up along coasts, with some nations insisting that fishing rights up to 200 miles offshore are theirs exclusively.

The present world fish catch includes freshwater species as well as mollusks (clams, oysters, scallops) and crustaceans (lobsters, crabs, shrimps). If the total fish catch is to grow, most of the increase will come not from the kinds of seafood we already know, but from species that are not usually harvested.

Many tons of edible fish are now wasted because they are not yet popular as food. Shrimp boats in the Gulf of Mexico catch fish in their nets and throw them away. For every pound of shrimp taken, between five and ten pounds

Sardinelike anchovies (left) are processed into fish meal that is eaten by chickens and livestock, but not by people.

of fish are caught. The most abundant species is croaker, a tasty fish which is not marketed in the United States. Other little-used seafood includes hake, shark, skate, squid, and king mackerel.

Past estimates of potential fish catch ran as high as 500 million metric tons. We now know that such a goal is out of the question. However, much more food can be harvested from the sea if we feed lower on food chains. Most of the fish now eaten are predators, at the top of food chains. They themselves eat smaller fish, crustaceans, and tiny organisms called plankton. If we ate from the same place on the food chain, much more food energy and nutrients would be available to us.

So far, the main research effort in this direction has been aimed at the krill—a shrimplike crustacean about two and a half inches long that lives in the Antarctic Ocean. American scientists estimate the total krill population at anywhere from 500 million metric tons to 4 billion metric tons. It is the biggest source of animal protein left in the world.

The Soviet Union harvested 200,000 metric tons of krill in 1974. It is trying to develop world markets for "cheese" spread and other krill foods. There is already concern about overfishing of krill. Such animals as whales, seals, penguins, terns, fish, and squid depend on krill for food. If markets for krill are developed, overfishing must be avoided for the sake of these animals as well as for people.

Any estimate of future food from the sea must take into account the effects of pollution. The oceans are our wastebaskets. They're big wastebaskets, but they cannot absorb and dilute poisonous substances forever. The greatest damage occurs along coasts and in estuaries, which are the most productive seafood areas and the "nurseries" of future fish populations. About 1 million tons of oil are spilled each year, and this amount will rise as oil tanker

All life in the ocean depends on the tiny phytoplankton at the bottom of the food pyramid. Most of the food energy in plankton is lost before it reaches humans in the seafood they eat. The oceans can provide people with much more food if we find ways to harvest small crustaceans and make them palatable.

A FOOD PYRAMID

traffic and offshore drilling increase. It may be foolish to expect greater food harvests from the sea while this sort of pollution continues.

Seafood is especially important in the world food situation because it is high-quality protein. Other sources of additional protein are now being investigated.

In 1974, the National Academy of Sciences searched the tropics for edible plants. One discovery, the winged bean, shows great promise. It is a high-protein plant and is superior to the soybean because nearly all of the winged bean (pods, beans, leaves, flowers, shoots, and tubers) is edible. If developed as a major crop, the winged bean may provide badly needed protein for people in the humid tropics.

Protein can also be squeezed out of alfalfa leaves and processed into a white powder. The powder can be used as flour or added to other foods. Certain kinds of yeasts can be grown on wastepaper or other organic wastes, then harvested as "single-cell protein." Such material so far has been used as livestock food. Whether it can be made safe and appealing for people is still in doubt.

New food sources like these might be called "protein in the sky." They are expensive, and most are still in the experimental stage. So far none of the new foods have been produced in large amounts priced low enough for the poor people who need them most. It is too early to dismiss these new kinds of foods, but we should avoid fooling ourselves about their usefulness in the present food crisis.

The crisis will only be solved by growing more grain, especially in the developing nations that need it most. The food policies of past decades must be changed. Developing nations must invest more of their own money and effort in food production, rather than in industrialization. And foreign aid must also change. As late as 1974, only 18 percent of World Bank loans went to agricultural projects. Developing nations need help in order to become self-sufficient in grains. This means providing not only high-yield seeds but also other forms of aid which will make the use of the seeds a real possibility for poor farmers.

"I have a lot of respect for the small farmer," said Dr. Norman Borlaug. "Almost invariably when you look at what he's doing with his land, you find he's producing the maximum under the situation he has to work with. The thing is that he usually doesn't have much to work with."

A peasant usually grows several grain varieties and crops on his plot of land. His yields may be low, but he almost always produces *something*. Planting his whole plot to a

new kind of seed and borrowing money to buy fertilizer are huge risks for him to take. Low-cost loans and other help must reduce the risk, because the hopes of feeding most of humankind rest on all the small farmers and their families, who make up at least a third of all people on earth.

It is especially important that the Green Revolution reach the poorest farmers with small plots of land. Rural unemployment and malnutrition would decrease, and the people would then feel it is "safe" to have fewer babies. And there may be a hidden bonus. Evidence from Mexico, India, South Korea, and Taiwan shows that small farms produce greater yields per acre than larger ones with absentee owners which are operated by tenant workers. Small family farms are worked more intensively, and the crops are given better care.

Any government program which emphasizes mechanized agriculture on large farms is inviting trouble. It is encouraging that the World Bank and AID have now aimed their programs at the problems of small farmers and rural development. Developing nations have a tremendous resource in idle manpower. Agricultural development which provides jobs will reduce overall poverty and will also help solve problems other than that of the food supply.

These ideas were among the many discussed at the 1974 United Nations World Food Conference. The conference ended on a note of optimism and doubt—optimism because some ways of solving the world food crisis were pointed out; and doubt that much would be done about them. For example, nearly all the food experts agreed that a world food reserve should be set up. But doing this is another matter.

The basic idea of an international food reserve, first pro-

"—Then too, we considered a revised resolution setting up a special fund providing a channel through which, hopefully, the oil producing countries as well as the exporting nations would contribute enough money and expertise to, oh, in say three or four years begin really massive shipments of grain...."

posed in the 1940s, is to buy grain in times of surplus and release it in years of scarcity. The reserve would be a buffer against famine and would keep grain prices within the reach of developing nations.

Such a reserve is probably in the best interests of all nations, but it has been opposed by most farmers, grain traders, and government leaders in the United States and Canada—the source of most of the world's surplus grain. The food reserve would probably keep grain prices from falling very low in times of abundance, but it would also tend to keep prices from rising very high in times of scarcity, and this did *not* appeal to the grain exporters. Almost every food expert agrees that the creation of an international grain reserve is a good idea, but economic and political obstacles may keep it from happening.

With or without an international food reserve, the surpluses of the United States and other grain-exporting nations will play the major role in averting future famine. But suppose there isn't enough grain to go around? Then if emergency grain is sent to all needy nations, none will get enough, and all will suffer from starvation or even famine. On the other hand, if all the grain is sent to a few nations, famine can be averted in them, but the other countries will suffer. How do you decide where to send the grain?

Will we have to decide which peoples should get emergency food, and which peoples will be allowed to starve?

Questions like these were raised by Dr. Garrett Hardin, an ecologist at the University of California. His answers are based on what he calls "lifeboat ethics." The developed nations of the world, he wrote, are adrift in lifeboats. "In the ocean outside each lifeboat swim the poor of the world, who would like to get in, or at least to share some of the wealth. What should the lifeboat passengers do? We could try to take everyone aboard, but we would sink the lifeboat if we did. The boat swamps, everyone drowns. Complete justice, complete catastrophe."

Dr. Hardin believes that we should not take everyone aboard. "For the foreseeable future," he concluded, "our survival demands that we govern our actions by the ethics of the lifeboat, harsh though they may be."

Dr. Hardin has said that we would be doing a favor to some starving nations as well as ourselves if we refused to send them food. He believes that it does more harm than good to send food to a nation that does not reduce its population growth. The problem itself remains unchanged by the food aid, and later on when another food shortage develops, there are even more people in need of rescue. This has been called "incubating [a] catastrophe." In this grim view of the future, the only choice seems to be between famine now and famine later, with more suffering, death, and damage to the environment if the famine occurs later.

Another scientist, Dr. Philip Handler, president of the National Academy of Sciences, has also said that lifeboat ethics make sense, but *only* if developed nations do not intend to first try a "colossal all-out effort" to help developing nations help themselves. He questions the wisdom of sending food aid to South Asia, where populations are expected to double by the year 2000. Unless some way is found to do a better job of helping than we do now, he said, "we are in very serious danger of doing something which, while soothing our consciences, may lead to the greatest debacle in all of history."

The idea of lifeboat ethics brought a storm of angry responses. Many people felt that it was cruel and inhumane to even consider "cutting Asia adrift," and to deliberately do nothing while people starved. A hopeful response came from Frances Moore Lappé, author of a book called *Diet for a Small Planet.* She wrote: "The first maxim of nautical ethics is that you don't go to the lifeboats, which will save only a few, until you've made every effort to salvage the ship for the sake of all."

Frances Lappé believes that aid from developed nations has not failed, but simply hasn't been tried on a scale that will really make a difference. She urges that developed nations spend much more to help developing nations to become self-sufficient in food. If the aid is massive enough, fast enough, and sensible enough, the question of lifeboat ethics need never be faced.

In actual practice, most of the U.S. aid of free or inexpensive food has seldom gone to the neediest nations anyway. Most of it was sent to such countries as South Vietnam, South Korea, Egypt, and others we considered to be political allies. And the United States cannot pretend that it has provided its share of other kinds of aid, such as fertilizer and agricultural advice. A dozen other industrial nations

spend a greater proportion of their budgets on foreign aid. It seems that a new, more generous spirit is needed in the United States.

Americans are facing other ethical questions, especially about the tremendous difference in diet between developed and developing nations. We used to say, "Clean your plate; people are starving in India." This is no longer enough; it never was. Reducing food waste is important, but this does not necessarily increase food supplies elsewhere. One thing we can do is change the kind and amount of aid to poor nations. Until recently, most foreign aid treated only the symptoms of the sick agriculture in developing nations. Another, more difficult task is to change our lifestyle and set a new example for the world.

We waste great amounts of resources and energy. American-style agriculture is particularly wasteful. It depends on fossil fuels, not human labor. It uses much more energy than it yields in food, beginning with the large amounts used to make and apply fertilizer, and including energy used for

Corn harvest is highly mechanized; this machine picks corn ears and removes the kernels from the cobs.

transportation, processing, grinding, freezing, baking, and so forth.

In 1970, about 2.9 million kilocalories of energy were needed to raise an acre of corn. This equals eighty gallons of gasoline. If manure had been substituted for commercial fertilizer, 1.1 million kilocalories of energy (equal to thirty gallons of gasoline) would have been saved. As supplies of fossil fuels dwindle and become more costly, we will have to find more energy-efficient ways to grow food.

Waste occurs at every point in food production and use, from the field to the table. For example, each year the United States produces 22 billion pounds of whey—a by-product when milk is made into cheese. Only a third of the whey is made into foods for people and animals. The rest is discarded. If it was dried and processed, it would yield vitamins, at least 170 million pounds of protein, and a billion pounds of milk sugar.

During food harvest and processing, millions of tons of useful leftovers are buried in landfills, burned, or dumped into waterways. And the waste continues in kitchens and dining rooms. At an elementary school in California, the contents of one cafeteria trash can were examined. It contained forty-one sandwiches, two cartons of milk, two pieces of chicken, nineteen apples, thirteen oranges, four carrots, two boxes of raisins, and fourteen cookies.

In Tucson, Arizona, a group of college students studied the garbage from hundreds of homes as it was brought to a landfill. They found that the average Tucson family threw away between 10 and 20 percent of the food they bought. The students estimated that Tucson citizens throw out 9,500 tons of edible food, worth $9 to $11 million, each year. (The garbage also included an estimated 80 million aluminum cans, worth about $470,000 if turned in at local recycling centers.)

Some people believe that the whole American diet will have to change. A good beginning would be to eat less meat, and especially less beef. Americans eat at least twice the amount of meat their bodies can use. Since our bodies can't store protein, the extra is excreted or used as energy. Most of it goes to waste, and therefore so does all the land, water, fertilizer, and fuel used to produce the beef. Livestock-raising is often terribly wasteful of many resources, including water. The "water cost" of a pound of beef is about twenty-five times that of a pound of bread.

More than half of the grain grown in the United States is used to feed livestock. In times of food scarcity, cattle and hogs compete with people in developing nations for avail-

able supplies of corn and soybeans. These animals do not have to be raised on grains. In fact, cattle are able to get nutrients and energy from feed that people can't use—grass, for instance. Cattle can also be raised on crop wastes and even on their own manure (after processing).

Many people have the notion that lots of meat is necessary for a healthy diet. But Americans are no more healthy than people in nations where much less meat is eaten. Most medical authorities believe that the rising rate of heart disease in the United States is linked to a diet of fatty meats. The American Heart Association recommends a one-third cut in meat consumption. Indeed, some experts on human nutrition now believe that a person who eats too much meat can be called malnourished.

The trend during the 1960s and early 1970s, however, was to grain-feed cattle in feed lots, the better to produce fat-rich beef. Twice as much energy is needed to produce a pound of fat than is needed to make a pound of lean, red meat. A lot of fat (an estimated 2.5 billion pounds) is trimmed off even before people buy the meat. More is trimmed off when the meat is prepared and eaten. An ounce here, a pound there—it adds up to a colossal waste. For health reasons it makes sense not to eat much fat, but it makes even more sense not to use grain to produce fatty meats in the first place.

For the sake of their own health, then, if not for other reasons, Americans should eat less beef. This need not wipe out the cattle industry. The United States has millions of acres of land that is not suited for raising grains but is fine for grazing. On this land, cattle are "walking protein factories," converting grass and other forage into meat rather efficiently—and into meat with less fat than that of grain-fed cattle. (People who are accustomed to the taste of grain-fed beef would soon adapt to the taste of grass-fed beef.)

Hogs and chickens are even more efficient (and contain less fat). If Americans simply ate more chicken and less beef, some land now used for raising cattle feed could be used to grow grains for export. And if total meat consumption in the United States was cut by only 10 percent, 12 million tons of grain now fed to livestock would become available.

Of course there is no guarantee that this grain would feed starving people. Instead, it might become part of a huge surplus that would drive grain prices down, reduce farmers' incomes, and cause them to plant less grain the following year. Likewise, if Americans use less fertilizer, there is no guarantee that a peasant in Asia will get more. Fertilizer manufacturers have to make a profit too. Someone has to pay for their products; someone has to pay for shipping fertilizer to developing nations.

The world food situation is complex. We can only guess at all the possible effects if Americans should change their diets and ways of farming.

One of the most positive effects would be the new example set by the United States. Our lifestyle is considered an ideal to strive for by many people in developing nations. Increasing numbers of Americans realize what a poor ideal it is. It is a lifestyle based on waste of all resources: energy, food, water, land. Our diet is definitely not a model of good nutrition.

If we have the good sense and the will to change to a less wasteful lifestyle, we will provide a new model for the millions of people who want to emulate us. And that, perhaps even more than surplus grain, will be a powerful force in our efforts to solve the world food crisis.

According to historians, 25 million people starved to death in the nineteenth century. In the twentieth century, "only" 12 million have starved—so far. What will the total be at the end of this century? It is within our power to choose the number. We know what we have to do in order to reduce population growth and produce enough food for everyone on earth. Now we must commit ourselves to this great task.

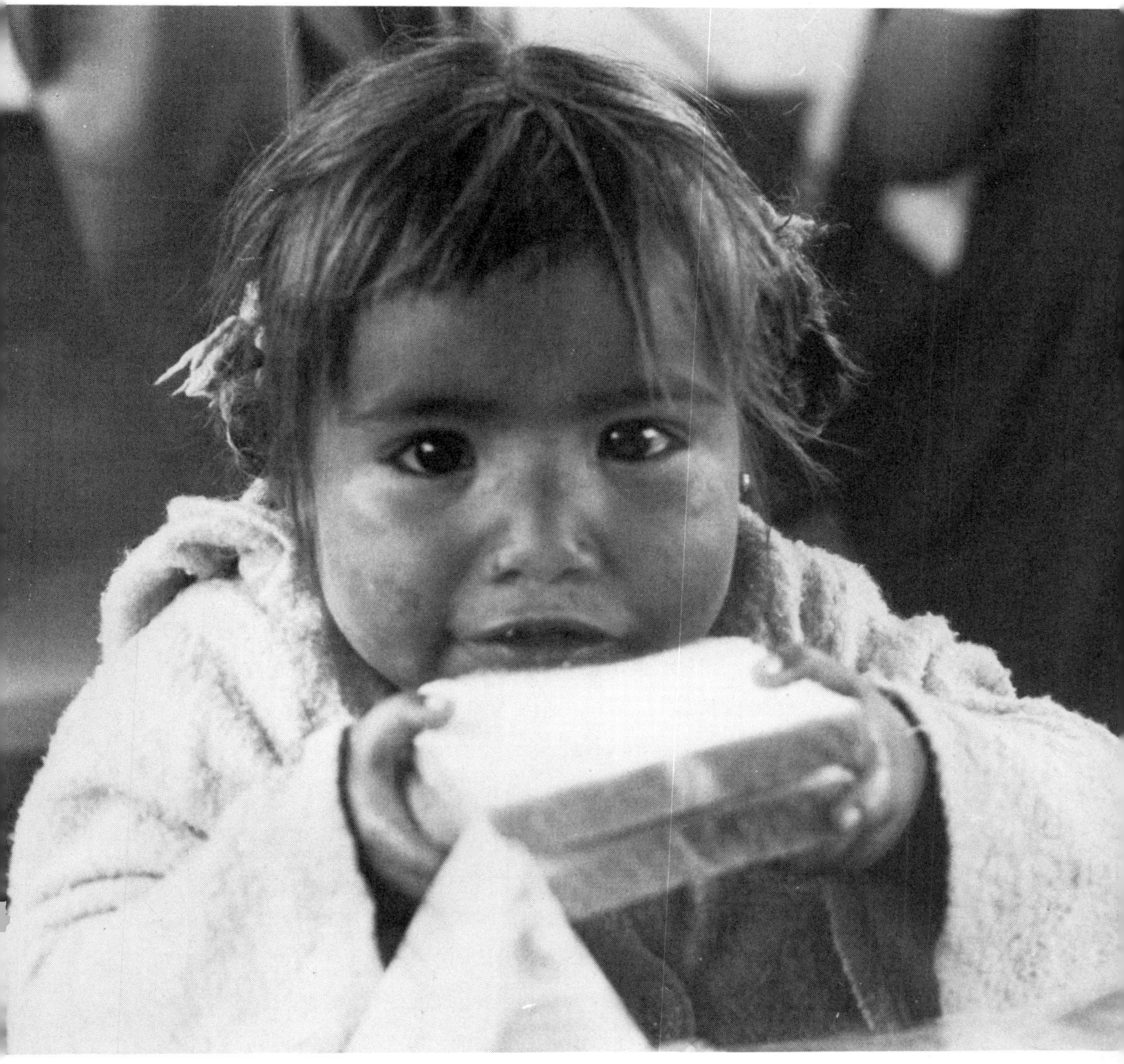

# GLOSSARY

AGRONOMY—the science of soil management and food plant production.

AMINO ACIDS—compounds consisting mostly of nitrogen, hydrogen, oxygen, and carbon, and which make up protein. More than 30 amino acids are known, and 22 are essential to human health. Of these, eight must be acquired directly from the food we eat.

ARABLE LAND—land that is fit for cultivation (from a Latin word meaning "to plow").

BIOCIDES—"life killers"; chemical poisons intended to kill plant and animal pests. Sometimes called pesticides, insecticides, or herbicides, but these substances kill beneficial organisms as well as pests.

CALORIE—a unit of heat energy. The calorie used to measure energy in our food is the large calorie or kilocalorie: equal to the amount of heat needed to raise the temperature of 1 kilogram of water by 1° Celsius. Most people in the United States need between 2,000 and 3,000 of these calories each day.

DEMOGRAPHIC TRANSITION—a process by which a human population changes from conditions of high birth and death rates to low birth and death rates. During the transition there is a population "explosion" because birth rates remain high for a while after death rates decline.

DEMOGRAPHY—the study of human populations: their size, distribution, behavior, make-up, and patterns of movement.

DESERTIFICATION—the process by which people change once-fertile land into barren desert, through overgrazing, removal of protective plant growth, or other abuse of the land.

DEVELOPED NATION—an industrialized nation, most of whose citizens have good health care, opportunities for education, and a high standard of living. Also called a rich nation, industrial nation, highly developed nation, or overdeveloped nation.

DEVELOPING NATION—a nation with little industrial development, most of whose citizens have low incomes and a low standard of living. Also called a poor nation or less developed nation.

ECONOMICS—the study of the production, distribution, and use of goods.

ESTUARY—a place where salt water and fresh water mix, usually where a river enters an ocean. Estuaries are among the most productive food sources on earth.

EUTROPHICATION—the process by which a body of water becomes enriched with minerals and other nutrients.

FALLOWING—the farming practice of leaving crop land idle for a period (usually a year) in order to maintain soil fertility and moisture; especially important in semiarid regions.

FAMINE—a great scarcity of food throughout an entire nation or region, resulting in widespread starvation.

FOSSIL FUELS—petroleum, coal, and natural gas (as well as fuels made from them, such as gasoline and kerosene). For the most part, they were formed more than 300 million years ago.

IRRIGATE—to supply land with water, usually through use of canals, ditches, flooding, or spraying.

LEGUME—a member of the plant family *Leguminosae,* which includes peas, beans, vetch, clover, and alfalfa. Bacteria living on the roots of these plants are capable of removing nitrogen gas from the air and converting it into nitrogen compounds that plants need for good growth.

MALNOURISHED—lacking a balanced diet of nutrients, including protein, fat, carbohydrates, vitamins, and minerals.

METEOROLOGY—the study of the earth's atmosphere, including weather and climate.

MONSOONS—wind systems that affect large regions and which reverse direction seasonally—for example, the monsoon that produces wet and dry seasons in India and southern Asia.

MUTATION—a new characteristic or trait of an organism which can be passed on to the next generation through reproduction. Most mutations are not useful or advantageous to the species of plant or animal. Some are useful: for example, a mutation of a wheat plant that would enable it (and future generations of wheat plants) to resist the attack of a pest.

PLANKTON—tiny, drifting plants and animals that live in salt and fresh water. The plant plankton (phytoplankton) include diatoms and algae. The animal plankton (zooplankton) include rotifers and copepods.

PROTEINS—complex chemical compounds, made up of amino acids, which occur in all living matter. Proteins are needed for normal growth, development, and maintenance of our bodies.

UNDERNOURISHED—lacking enough food calories to meet minimum energy needs.

VITAMINS—compounds which living things need in small amounts for normal growth and development. They cannot be manufactured in the body, and must be obtained from food.

# FURTHER READING

*Books and magazines marked with an asterisk (*) are fairly simple; the others are more difficult.*


*BERG, ALAN, "To Save the World from Lifeboats." *Natural History,* June–July 1975, pp. 4–6. An expert on nutrition criticizes the notion of "lifeboat ethics."

*BROWN, LESTER R., *By Bread Alone.* New York: Praeger Publishers, 1974. Brown's assessment of the world food situation in the mid-1970s, including his optimistic projection of reduced population growth.

*———, *Seeds of Change.* New York: Praeger Publishers, 1970. An enthusiastic account of the early promise of the Green Revolution, with warnings about problems which have since developed.

———, "The World Food Prospect." *Science,* 12 December 1975, pp. 1053–1059. "In the future," Brown concludes, "scarcity may be more or less persistent, relieved only by sporadic surpluses."

*CANBY, THOMAS, "Can the World Feed Its People?" *Na-*

*tional Geographic*, July 1975, pp. 2–31. A richly illustrated article that touches many facets of the world food problem.

*ECKHOLM, ERIK, *Losing Ground: Environmental Stress and World Food Prospects*. New York: W. W. Norton & Company, 1975. The present and potential environmental costs of food production.

*———, "Salting the Earth." *Environment*, October 1975, pp. 9–15. Salt deposits from irrigation water may lessen the productivity of at least one-third of the earth's irrigated land.

GROTH, EDWARD, "Increasing the Harvest." *Environment*, January–February 1975, pp. 28–39. Food production in the United States can be increased, but there will be environmental costs.

*LAPPÉ, FRANCES MOORE, *Diet for a Small Planet*. New York: Ballantine Books, revised 1975. A 412-page paperback book which describes our excessive use of meat, and gives a plan and recipes for improved nutrition.

*MILLER, JUDITH, "Genetic Erosion: Crop Plants Threatened by Government Neglect." *Science*, 21 December 1973, pp. 1231–1233. Genetic variety of crop plants is being lost, and not much is being done about it.

PIMENTAL, DAVID, *et al.*, "Food Production and the Energy Crisis." *Science*, 2 November 1973, pp. 443–449. Crop production in the United States, and in the Green Revolution, depends heavily on fossil fuels, which will become scarce and more expensive.

*PRINGLE, LAURENCE, *Energy: Power for People*. New York:

Macmillan Publishing Co., Inc., 1975. Includes details about the huge waste of energy in the American life-style.

*———, *One Earth, Many People.* New York: Macmillan Publishing Co., Inc., 1971. The effects of population growth on the earth's resources, and prospects for reaching zero population growth.

*———, *Pests and People: The Search for Sensible Pest Control.* New York: Macmillan Publishing Co., Inc., 1972. The use and misuse of chemical biocides, and alternatives to them.

REVELLE, ROGER, "Food and Population." *Scientific American,* September 1974, pp. 160–170. A population expert argues that increased food production will help create conditions leading to a halt in population growth.

SANDERSON, FRED H., *et al., Food: Politics, Economics, Nutrition, and Research.* Washington, D.C.: American Association for the Advancement of Science, 1975. More than 20 scientific articles about various opportunities and obstacles of the world food situation.

*SEBRELL, WILLIAM H., JR., and HAGGERTY, JAMES J., *Food and Nutrition* (LIFE Science Library). New York: Time-Life Books, 1967. A heavily illustrated introduction to nutrition, vitamins, and food production in the United States and the rest of the world.

*WADE, NICHOLAS, "Sahelian Drought: No Victory for Western Aid." *Science,* 19 July 1974, pp. 234–237. How foreign aid helped bring about the Sahelian famine of the early 1970s.

# INDEX

*Asterisk (*) indicates photograph or drawing*

PICTURE CREDITS: Ian R. Gilbert, 12; *Newsweek* (Jeff Lowenthal), 103; Laurence Pringle, 90 (both), 106; Rockefeller Foundation, 42; Santa Fe Railway, 9; David Sumner, 50; Union Carbide, vi; United Nations, 11, 23, 27, 31, 41, 45, 49, 52, 55, 60, 70, 78, 79, 83, 101; United Nations/FAO, 3, 6, 20, 22, 24, 38, 46, 53, 64, 67, 73, 92, 93, 109; United Nations/ILO, 28, 34–35; UNICEF, 16; U.S. Department of Agriculture, 5, 7, 57 (both), 59, 62 (both), 66, 68–69, 72, 76, 77, 80, 82, 86, 104; Richard Willson, 17; Don Wright, 99. Drawings by Erick Ingraham: 15, 30, 37, 39, 75, 88, 95.